LIVING IN CHRIST

BY TERRY MATHEWS

Living in Christ
ISBN: 978-1-939570-98-7

Published by Word and Spirit Publishing
P.O. Box 701403
Tulsa, Oklahoma 74170
wordandspiritpublishing.com

TABLE OF CONTENTS

CHAPTER 1:

LIVING IN CHRIST

I believe you're at the right place at the right time, and God's going to do something wonderful in all of our lives, mine included, as we study who we are in Christ Jesus. To me that's one of the most profound revelations of the New Testament. It's not just what happened *to* Christ on the cross that changes us, although, it does; but it's what happened *in* Christ on the cross that changes us.

We're going to go farther than we've ever been before in understanding what was really happening in the mind of God when Jesus went to Calvary. He took our sin. He took our shame. He went in our place. So now, because of that, we have what He's got, and we're going to study that together.

I'm so glad you picked up this book. It is a great opportunity for me to share with you what Christ has put in my heart. I live in Albuquerque, New Mexico. I pastored a church there for thirty-two years. When I thought about writing this book, I was a little hesitant at first. It's such a powerful truth that needs to be communicated, but I wondered if I could share it well enough. I began to pray, and this is what the Lord said to me: "You have a good foundation in the new creation realities. This will be an opportunity for you to go deeper and to take others with you." He was speaking about *you*!

The Lord also said that not only will I take others with me, but that He would help me communicate His message. So, when I heard Him say that, I said, "I'm in! I'll do exactly what You want me to do."

I believe God has given me a divine commission and the help and grace I need to minister life into you and strengthen you in this reality of who we are in Christ Jesus. We are who the Bible says we are. We can do what the Bible says we can do. We can have what the Bible says we can have. So, my heart is that together we will shake some things up and wake up new revelation within us as we read this book. I desire that we stand up to new heights and dimensions in Christ Jesus until, as the Bible says, we come to the fullness of the stature of Christ. (Ephesians 4:13)

LIFE IN CHRIST

There's a great Scripture I want you to see in 1 Corinthians 15:22. This will be a foundational Scripture, as well as a few others. It says, *"For as in Adam all die, even so in Christ shall all be made alive."*

We're going to talk about our *life in Christ*—who we are in Him, who He is in us. We're going to come to know the fact that we are not just repaired or worked over. We are made *brand new* through the power of the Holy Spirit. The death, burial, and resurrection of Jesus meant something to us then, and it means something to us now. We are a new species of being in Christ. We are God-people, love-people, Jesus-people, and God's going to help us come to a deeper understanding of this than we have ever had before.

As we embark on this journey into knowing who we are in Christ in a deeper way, it will absolutely change everything. We are not just sinners saved by grace. We *were* sinners. We got saved by grace. **Now we have become the very righteousness of God in Christ.** We're going to dig into that and understand what this righteousness *means*.

This book will paint a whole new picture. And hopefully, we'll begin to see what the Father saw and walk in a new creation reality for ourselves. Praise God! Hallelujah! Thank you, Jesus! Amen!

MY STORY

Let me tell you a little bit about my story—how I'm here and why I'm here. My wife and I were born again, received Jesus as our Lord and Savior in 1970. We were in Chicago playing music in a nightclub in 1970. We were not born again, and we were not Christians. I had some church background. My dad was an Assembly of God pastor, and my brother went to an Assembly of God Bible school. I, on the other hand, chose to go the way of the world. I liked to play music—rhythm and blues and rock-n-roll. I also liked to make money, and really, it took me downhill. That was until God lifted me out by His grace and mercy and set me free.

In 1970, on a Saturday night before Easter Sunday, we were getting ready to go play music in the Palmer House Hotel in downtown Chicago. We lifted up our hearts and said, "Jesus, would you come into our lives?" I prayed a simple prayer like that.

My wife's name is Angel. Isn't that a great name? I married an "Angel." I tell people I wake up with an Angel in my bedroom every morning!

Before we got married, Columbia Records was looking at Angel to do a demo record. I was spending time really looking for God and seeking after God. The tension in our life was pretty heavy. One reason I prayed that prayer was because our relationship was really strained. Neither one of us were saved. So that night when we prayed that prayer, the life and love of God filled that place, and we became born-again believers. We left Chicago and got married about three or four months later.

In all the traveling I did with the musicians and living that lifestyle, I had really gone deeper and deeper away from God. Thank God for my momma and all the others who were praying for me—God was really getting my attention. If I had listened, I really feel I wouldn't have had to go through what I went through. Sadly, however, I wouldn't listen at first.

In 1969, I got picked up on a drug charge in Kansas City, Kansas. They put us in jail in Olathe, Kansas. While we were out of jail on bail, I got permission from the judge to help a friend of mine move from Chicago to LA. He was a band-booking agent from Chicago, and I got permission to help him.

We drove from Chicago to LA and went right through Albuquerque, New Mexico. I had never been to Albuquerque. I never knew it even existed. We were on Route 66, going all the way to California, and we stopped in Albuquerque to spend the night with his brother. His brother happened to be a Baptist, a born-again believer.

While we were staying at his house, he asked us to go to a prayer meeting by the university.

I really didn't want to go to the prayer meeting, but we were staying all night with him, so you do what they tell you to do. We went to the prayer meeting. I walked into this barely 1,200 square foot home by the University of New Mexico, and I saw young people turned on to Jesus! They called those days the "Jesus Movement" days. Kids were getting saved by the thousands! I walked into this little house, and here was a group of college kids and high school kids who were *on fire*. Some of them were praying together. Some of them were just fellowshipping and having a cup of coffee. Others were sitting down and looking at the Bible. I knew that it was different. I knew God was there, but even though it influenced my life, I did not make a commitment to Christ.

We went on to LA the next day. From there, I flew back to Kansas City to go stand before the judge in Olathe, Kansas, which was the county seat. When I stood before the judge, he dropped my charges from a felony to a misdemeanor. Praise the Lord for that! However, he did give me one year in the county jail. This was crazy. Although I had broken the law, I'd never been in jail or been in trouble like that before. I went straight to jail.

I didn't know this until ten years later, but the judge had actually called my mother. The judge told my mother, "I'm going to put your boy in jail for thirty days. He doesn't have a record, but there's something about him, and I feel like he needs to get away from that whole lifestyle and those he's running with for a while. Maybe this will help him."

I didn't know that. I thought I had to do at least ninety days before I could get paroled. So there I was in jail, and God was dealing with me. I began to talk to God. I said, "You know, this is what I'll do. I'll read Matthew, Mark, Luke, and John. I'll read about Jesus." Remember, I had a church background—Sunday morning, Sunday night, Wednesday night—but I hadn't committed to Christ. And I did just that. For thirty days, I read the four Gospels and reread them. Something began to happen to me. I didn't make a commitment in jail, but God was definitely working on me.

They ended up letting me out in thirty days. We smoked a joint on the way home from jail! It looked like nothing had changed, but something was happening inside. You know what was happening? God was getting a hold of my life! Praise the Lord!

After I got out of jail, I went and picked up Angel in December of 1969 and drove to Chicago, and that's how we ended up in Chicago under a sixteen-week contract at the Palmer House Hotel. That's where we were.

So I kept my commitment to God. I kept reading Matthew, Mark, Luke, and John, even after I got to Chicago. Even after we were playing in the nightclub, I kept reading the Word. **The Word of God is powerful!** It began to change my life. Something began to happen to me. I hadn't committed to Christ yet, but I thought, *Whoa! Something good is going on!* I'm reading about Jesus and His love for people and what He did and what He said. At this point, I was really getting filled up spiritually, and my life began to change.

So, I read in the Bible where Jesus said, "*When you pray, get in your closet and pray*" (Matthew 6:6, paraphrased). I thought He really meant get in the clothes closet. So that's what I did. I just got in the clothes closet, and I'd go in there with a can of beer, a joint, and my Bible. Sounds like a good book, doesn't it? I kept drinking the beer and smoking the weed, but I was reading the Bible. And guess what? The Word of God began to win out—less booze, less weed, and more Bible; less booze, less weed, more Bible!

This was the whole scenario that was happening in our lives. After fourteen weeks in Chicago, the Saturday night before Easter Sunday, when our relationship was being really stretched. I'd been reading about Jesus, and that night, in the midst of that tension-filled room, I lifted my hands, and I said, "Jesus, would you come into our lives?" The light of God hit that place. Angel and I both began to weep as Christ touched our lives and we became born-again believers. I looked at Angel that very moment, and I said, "Angel, something's happened to us. We're leaving Chicago, and I'm going to Albuquerque to preach the Gospel."

God was dealing with me right away that Albuquerque was my destination. That's the only place I knew. He said, "That'll be your destiny. You go and preach the Gospel." How was I going to preach the Gospel? All I knew was that I was reading about Jesus, and I had lifted my hands—but that's what we did. We left Chicago and went home. Angel and I separated for three or four months, but then we got married in the summer of 1970 and headed to Albuquerque. There, I called a ministry on the phone, and I said, "I've given my life to Jesus, and I want to come and do what you're doing."

They said, "Come on." We headed to Albuquerque with $60 in our pocket and everything we owned in a '67 Camaro! I'd still like to have that car!

We went to Albuquerque with a love for Jesus and a love for each other. We showed up on the front porch of that ministry center. The little 1,200-square foot ministry house had expanded, and now they were in a fourteen-room log cabin in downtown Albuquerque in Highland Park. They had taken the whole facility over, and they were ministering to hippies and hitchhikers and college kids and high school kids, and they were telling them about Jesus.

They welcomed Angel and me in, and we shared our testimony; that's all we knew to do. We'd also play a few songs. I knew a lot of church songs, so I'd jazz them up a little bit, and we'd sing about Jesus. And people were getting saved! It was wonderful!

MENTORED BY KENNETH HAGIN

Now, here's what happened. One day a couple showed up at the ministry center with a reel-to-reel tape. There were no CDs then; this was 1970. A reel-to-reel tape and a tape player—a big one—by a man named Kenneth Hagin. I'd never heard of Kenneth Hagin. The name of the tape was *Paul's Revelation*. They let them play that big reel-to-reel tape in the meeting room of that log cabin to all the staff. I heard *who you are in Christ* for the first time in my life. I heard terms like "new creation realities," "understanding what Jesus did and why He did it," and "who we are because of it."

I just went wild! **It was like water to a thirsty man!** And I began to really follow after Brother Hagin. He became a spiritual father to me, though there was no Rhema Bible School yet. But through tapes, books, conferences, and conventions he fathered me, blessed my life, and I'll forever be grateful. I learned in the early '70s the truth about who we are in Christ.

Now here's what Brother Hagin said in the '70s: "Go through the New Testament, primarily Paul's letters, and underline every verse that you find that has the term 'in Christ,' 'in Him,' or 'in whom.'" He said there are approximately 130 of them. After you go through and underline them, he said, "Write them down." Then he said, "Confess them out loud, first-person singular." And then he said, "Say this, 'That is who I am, and that is what I have.'"

I started going through the New Testament looking up "in Him" Scriptures, "in Christ" Scriptures, and "in whom" Scriptures. That's new creation realities. **That's where the new creation is—in Christ.**

My wife and I would take those little 3x5 cards, and we'd have "confession sessions." That's what we called it in our little center. This couple that brought the message of faith and "in Christ" realities also brought the message of the baptism of the Holy Spirit. Because it was a Baptist-based organization and Angel and I received the Holy Spirit, they told us we would have to leave.

So we left in good standing. We moved into a little eight-foot wide mobile home where we would have our confession sessions declaring who we are in Christ. We got so excited studying new creation realities!

When the Lord said to me, "You have a good foundation in this," I knew what He was talking about because I really began my Christian walk in new creation realities. I would meditate on them, and I would speak them out. I would also sing them. And God would work in my life in a mighty way.

So, Angel and I left that ministry, went with this couple, and helped them start a church in Albuquerque. I became the praise and worship leader and served them for ten years. I also became the assistant pastor, and I owned a roofing company and made money roofing. We had a goin', blowin' church! In the '70s, if you had 200 to 300 people in a church, that was a big church. We had that many, particularly young people, turned on to God during the Jesus Movement days.

This is my background. I'm writing this book because God asked me to share what I know. He asked me to not only share what I know, but to go deeper than I've ever been before. He also said, "I want you to take somebody with you!" Then He said, "I will help you."

So, with that in mind, here's what I believe is going to happen: I'm going to help you, with the help of the Holy Spirit, to unlock your spiritual identity. You will never be the same because once we understand who we are in Christ and who Christ is in us, we are invincible! Praise the Lord! Hallelujah!

We're going to shake some things up. We're going to wake some things up. We're going to *stand up tall in Christ.*

START WITH PAUL

We're going to start with the book of Philippians chapter three. I want you to see something right at the beginning. The Apostle Paul in this chapter was really rehearsing who he was and talking about who he is after Christ. The whole chapter is a new creation reality chapter, by the way, but I just want to pick it up in verse eight and show you something. In verse eight he said this, "*Yea doubtless, and I count all things but loss for the excellency of the knowledge of Christ Jesus my Lord, for whom I have suffered the loss of all things, and do count them but rubbish, that I may win Christ.*"

Paul knew there was something in Christ that he needed to know. There's something he found out, but it just kept growing and going deeper than he'd ever been before.

Now when he says, "I've lost all things," he's talking about his former life as a Pharisee. He was so rigid in his walk. He was so ablaze with pharisaical doctrine that he persecuted Christians. And he just didn't talk about them. Actually, he killed some and put some in jail. But he said, "Look, I have come to realize that that's not where it's at. It's not about my own self-righteousness—what I can do to get God to approve of me. No. We can never do that."

Notice what he said in verse nine, "*And be found in Him* [there's that little phrase 'in Him'], *not having my own righteous-*

ness, which is from the law, but that which is through faith in Christ, the righteousness which is from God by faith."

I love that statement. He said, "That I may be found *in him*" (verse 9). New creation realities say we're going to find ourselves in Christ. You're going to find out something about yourself that you've never known before. And this revelation and this understanding will change everything. Praise God!

The thing that's so impressive about finding ourselves in Christ is this: at the writing of this chapter, the Apostle Paul had been in ministry approximately thirty years. Thirty years and he's still pursuing the things of Christ. He's still pursuing new creation realities. He's still pursuing an understanding of who Christ is, what Christ did, and who he is because of that. He wasn't slowing down! I like this! After thirty years, he is still passionate about knowing who he is in Christ, knowing Jesus better, knowing Him in a deeper way.

He uses this phrase, "I want to be found in Him." I want to be *found* in Him. Finding ourselves in Christ is so vital and so important. He goes on to say, "*My determined purpose is to know Christ, and the power of His resurrection, and the fellowship of His sufferings, being made conformable unto His death; that if by any means I might attain unto the resurrection of the dead*" (Philippians 3:10-11, paraphrased).

He said, "I'm looking at Christ, His life, His love, His death, burial, and resurrection." He said, "I know there's more there than I've found so far, and I'm not going to stop looking. I'm not going to stop seeking. I am going to continue finding out *who* I am *in Christ*, and *who Christ is in me*, and what He did brings total victory."

Look what he says in verse twelve: "*Not as though I had already attained, either were already perfect: but I follow after, if that I may apprehend that for which also I am apprehended of Christ Jesus.*" What does he mean? He's saying, "Look, I know there's more. I know there's more."

This may be the first time you've ever read a book about new creation realities. Maybe it's the first time you've even heard that term. I experienced that back in the '70s. I'd never heard a term "who you are in Christ," or "Paul's revelation," but I'm telling you, it began to change my life. It's still changing my life all these years later, and I'm going deeper. I'm going deeper than I've ever been before! Come on, let's go deeper together.

Paul is saying, "Look, I know there's more. I know there's more. Don't plateau. I mean, keep going. Keep digging. Keep looking. Keep seeking. Keep finding. Keep praising. Keep praying. Keep believing." He said, "Something has got a hold of me." He said, "I'm trying to apprehend, or get a grip on, what got a grip on me."

Does it have a grip on you?

BACK TO ACTS

Now, let's just take a little journey back to the Book of Acts. We'll come right back to Philippians, but I want you to see what he's talking about in his conversion in Acts nine. Paul the apostle was formerly called Saul of Tarsus. So in Acts 9:1 it says, "*And Saul, yet breathing out threatenings and slaughter against the disciples of the Lord, went unto the high priest.*"

So here's a guy who is so radical he is threatening and slaughtering and bringing Christians to prison. "And desired of him letters to Damascus to the synagogues, that if he found any of this way [talking about Christians], whether they were men or women, he might bring them bound unto Jerusalem" (Acts 9:2; brackets TM).

So here's a guy on a mission to put Christians in bonds, destroy their families and destroy their lives.

Notice verse three, "*And as he journeyed, he came near Damascus: and suddenly there shined round about him a light from heaven: And he fell to the earth, and heard a voice saying unto him, Saul, Saul, why persecutest thou me? And he said, Who art thou, Lord? And the Lord said, I am Jesus whom thou persecutest: it is hard for thee to kick against the pricks [cactus]. And he trembling and astonished said, Lord, what wilt thou have me to do? And the Lord said unto him, Arise, and go into the city, and it shall be told thee what thou must do*" (Acts 9:3-6, brackets TM).

Now that is the testimony of Paul's conversion. He was going against God's people, and Jesus appeared, and a light blinded him. He fell on the ground, and Jesus spoke to him. And even though he was a madman, he was smart enough to know when the Lord showed up. And he said, "What must I do, Lord?" Paul was converted right there. His name was Saul. I like to say Jesus knocked him off of that donkey he was riding so hard that it knocked the "S" off of his name and replaced it with a "P"! Saul became Paul—talk about a new creation! He got a new name. He got a new calling. He got a new life. And he wrote *two-thirds* of the New Testament.

So, in Philippians when Paul says, "I'm trying to get a grip on this that has got a grip on me," he said, "Something hit me hard and changed my life and called my name and set me free and I've got to find out more about Jesus." He continued to say, "Really, my life is *in Him*. And that's what I'm looking for, and that's what I'm going for."

So to be found in Him, to go deeper in Him, to let this message become—not only part of our life today but forever—we, like Paul, can say this: **"I'm still looking for more. I want to**

understand His love, His personality, His power, and His provision like never before."

Philippians 3:12 says, "*Not as though I had already attained, either were already perfect: but I follow after, if that I may apprehend that for which also I am apprehended of Christ Jesus.*" You'll find your purpose in Christ in the new creation realities.

Look at 3:13: "*Brethren, I count not myself to have apprehended...*" Remember, this is a man that had been in ministry for thirty years. That's impressive to me. I love it! He said, "After 30 years, I'm still as hungry as I've ever been for more of God. I want to know Him better."

He said, "*This one thing I do...*" Watch this. "*Forgetting those things which are behind...*" **You know, you can't go forward looking backward.** You can't go forward looking into yesterday. I believe that one of the greatest tricks of the devil is to cause us to get our eyes off of Jesus and to put them on ourselves and on our failures. Don't look back. Look to Jesus. He's the author and the finisher of our faith, and our life is in Him! We are new creatures in Christ! Hallelujah! Glory to God!

He said, "Look. This one thing I do." That's a good thing to do. Forget what's behind you. Don't stop there. Reach forward to the things that are before us (verse thirteen, paraphrased). There's a whole other world in Christ to discover.

Paul said, "I'm going to go forward, and I'm going to keep reaching." And then watch verse 14, "*I press toward the mark for the prize of the high calling of God* [where is it?] *in Christ Jesus*" (brackets TM). Hallelujah! I press toward the mark for the prize of the high calling of God in Christ Jesus. You see why he said after thirty years of ministry that he wanted to be found in Him was because he knew that's where the high calling, his high calling and ours, would be found in Jesus. The more we know about Jesus, the more we understand His plan and purpose, the more we grow in Christ. God is an awesome God and He is doing great things.

So I believe we're going to press on into the high calling of God in Christ Jesus. We're not going to just do this in this book and forget about it. It's a lifestyle.

FOUR PREPOSITIONS THAT WILL CHANGE YOUR LIFE

I don't know who said it, but I wrote this down way back in the '70s when I began to understand new creation realities: "The English language was not constructed for prepositions to carry the weight that the Gospel demands them to carry." This is so vital because we're talking about new creation realities, and this will help us to understand how that unfolds.

When I read that, I began to understand how it's so easy for us to overlook the prepositions. A preposition, as you probably know, is usually a little unnoticed word in front of a noun or pronoun that magnifies or expresses a relationship. We can read a whole verse and read right over a little preposition like "in." Yet that "in" Christ, that preposition, magnifies or expresses a relationship.

I learned this from Brother Hagin in the early '70s that these little prepositions cannot go unnoticed. The Gospel is a powerful truth to us from God, and these little prepositions bring to us an understanding of our relationship *to* Christ, or *with* Christ, or *in* Christ.

So primarily we're going to talk about four prepositions. Here they are: number one, "in." It means *union*. Any time you see *in*

Christ, *in* Him, *in* whom, that means in union with Him. I've been *united* to Him. Praise God, I'm one with Him in this life!

The second one is "with." "With" means *identification.* I was crucified *with* Christ. I was buried *with* Christ. I was raised *with* Christ. Now I'm seated *with* Christ. I've got a spiritual identification. Hallelujah! It's my spiritual identification. **Every time we see "with," we're going to think, *Wow, that's together with Christ.*** That's the same thing. I'm with Him in this. Identification is legal proof that you are who you say you are. **We've got legal proof from the Word of God that we are who God says we are, crucified with Christ, buried with Christ, raised with Christ, and seated with Christ.** That's who I am, that's what I have.

Don't be like that old boy down in the deep south. He got stopped by the highway patrol. The highway patrol pulled him over, walked up to the car, and said, "You got any I.D.?"

And the man said, "'Bout what?"

"You got any I.D.?"

"'Bout what?"

So when I tell you what your identification is "in Christ," don't be saying that you don't have any *idea* what I'm talking about. You go to the airport, they want your I.D. You've got to show them who you are—legal proof that you are who you say you are. We have the Word of God as a document that tells us who we are in Christ, which is our spiritual identification. Get to know it, and you will show it by the life that you live in Christ.

Here's another one, "for." The new creation realities are tied up in these little prepositions. The word "for" means: *substitution*, or *on our behalf.* He made Him to be sin *for* us. What? On our behalf as our substitute, that we might be made the righteousness of God in union with Him. I am connected and you are too—to Christ, to all He is, all He has, and all He's done. Praise God. Hallelujah!

And then the final one, the fourth one is the word "through." Or in some cases, it's translated "by"—*by* Christ, *through* Christ. That word means *function*. I function in this life through Him who loved me and gave Himself up for me. I *function* in life based on this new creation reality that I've come to understand through the power of these prepositions.

I wrote this down in my Bible years ago, "Because Jesus died *for* us, He was raised *for* us. He was seated *for* us. Then we died *with* Him. We're raised *with* Him. We're seated *with* Him, and now we're *in* Him." Hallelujah! I am connected! I've got friends in high places. His life is in me. So, through Him, and through this life, and through these new creation realities, I can function. I can live victoriously. I can have great expectation. **I can have marvelous hope and strength that can only come from the Lord Jesus Christ.**

We have been united to the Vine. Thank God, I'm His and He is mine. I have left the old nature far behind me. I have been grafted into the vine, one with Christ, united to Christ, raised with Christ, living in Christ, and because of that we have great expectation. We have great hope, and we thank God for it.

Sometimes these little words are just overlooked. I'm telling you, you're going to find Scriptures that you never knew were "in Him" reality Scriptures. We can't cover every Scripture that has "in Christ," "in Him," "in whom." But your job, like mine was back then, was to take time and go through those letters and underline or highlight those "in Him" Scriptures. Write them down. Those "in whom" Scriptures, write them down. Those "in Christ" Scriptures, write them down. Then, I recommend confessing them out: That's who I am. That's what I have. Speak them out in the first person singular.

We will cover many of them, but we won't get to all 130. You're going to get time alone with God to understand who you are in Him and how the reality of the power of the new creation will work in your life as never before. I believe new doors will open. I believe increase will come on every level—understanding, help, hope, and strength, because all of that is found in Christ.

EVERY GOOD THING

> One of our key Scriptures will be Philemon. It only has one chapter, and we will look at verse six. Get it down, because it's very important. I'll refer to it often. It says this, "*That the communication of thy faith may become effectual by the acknowledging of every good thing which is in you in Christ Jesus.*"

What does that mean? It means that as I take time to feed upon the Scriptures about the new creation realities and put them in my mouth, my faith and the communication of my faith becomes effectual, powerful, and sets me apart, as I begin to acknowledge who Jesus is and what Jesus has done.

Take time to look up some in Christ scriptures and begin to write them down and then begin to daily acknowledge "that's who I am" and "that's what I have."

CHAPTER 2:

HAPPY NEW YOU

I was traveling a few years ago. It happened to be on New Year's Day. And you know how you board the plane down the jetway, and the flight attendants welcome everybody, and they say "hi" as you come in. I could see her welcoming everybody in front of me as I was coming down the jetway. When she got to me, I think what she was wanting to say was, "Happy New Year to you," because it was New Year's Day. But when she looked at me, she said these words, "Happy new you." Happy new you! And of course, I started laughing, and she started laughing. But you know, I got a great charge out of that—happy new you! And so that's the name of our chapter—*Happy New You!*

I know it may or may not be New Year's Day as you read this—that's not the point. But I can tell you this—it's a new day for you today in God if you're a new creature in Christ Jesus. So happy new you!

We are going to be looking at 2 Corinthians 5:17 at two basic, fundamental new creation reality Scriptures. It says this: "*Therefore if any man* [meaning person, male or female] *be in Christ...*" Now that's an interesting term—if any person be *in*

Christ. Well, how in the world do you get *in Christ*? You'll remember in our last chapter, we talked about the power of prepositions. Remember that "in" speaks of union.

Another of our text Scriptures is 1 Corinthians 15:22, which says, "*In Adam all die...*" So, in Adam, because of Adam's sin, death came upon all people. *"For as in Adam all die, even so in Christ shall all be made alive."* So what Adam did affected everybody. But what *Jesus* did also affected everybody. Anybody can get *in Christ*, but let me tell you something—you can't buy your way in; you can't work your way in; you've got to *believe* your way in. Simply believe in Jesus as Lord and Savior and you are put in Christ.

One of my favorite "in Him" Scriptures is 1 Corinthians 1:30, which says, "*But of him are ye in Christ Jesus, who of God is made unto us wisdom, and righteousness, and sanctification, and redemption:*" I love that terminology, "*Of him are you in Christ.*" What does that mean? When I get born of God, I'm put into Christ. And God sees me in Christ. He sees us in Christ. He doesn't see what we used to be. He doesn't see us in our sin or our failures or all of that. He sees us in Christ.

Now those things affected us, but in Christ, the "new" has come. Victory has come. And we have a right to believe God for everything He says is ours in Christ. That's called "new creation realities." Hallelujah! Make it real!

AM I OR AREN'T I?

Let's go back to 2 Corinthians 5:17, which says, "*Therefore if any man be in Christ...*" How do I get "in Christ?" Through faith in the blood of Jesus. He said, "*...he is a new creature*" (verse 17). I like what it says in the margin of that in my Bible: "Therefore if any man be in Christ, let him *be* a new creature." Well, you say,

"Well, either I am, or I ain't." Well, you *are*, but you have to *let it be*. We have to cooperate with it. That's why you're reading this book. If you and I never take time to study "in Christ" realities, we probably will not let what *is* be in us now to the degree that God intended for it to be. You and I are not to be bound by circumstances, by sin, by the devil, or by anything. We have been set free! Happy new you! Praise God! **You are a new creature in Christ Jesus.**

Notice what he said, "Let it be." So let the new things be. Believe God. Speak out those new things. Take Philemon 1:6 and acknowledge every good thing that's in you in Christ.

When I learned this in the '70s from Brother Hagin, the "in Christ" realities, and I began to speak those out, my life radically changed. But here's the thing he said that blessed me most. He said, "I've seen Christians grow more in six months' time by speaking out 'in Christ' realities than other Christians have grown in years, ten years or more." He said, "There's something about knowing who we are in Christ that helps us develop into that full grown-spiritual man."

You say, "Well, will I ever get to a place where I don't need to go over any of those?" No. No, you won't. Like the Apostle Paul, who knew more about "in Christ" realities than any man on the planet, still said after thirty years, "I'm still trying to get a grip on these 'in Christ' realities. They're working in me, all right, but there's more. It's deeper!" He said, "I'm pressing toward the mark of the prize of the high calling of God that's in Christ Jesus!"

So, I'm saying, let's keep pressing. Let's keep searching. Let's keep looking. Let's keep finding ourselves in Christ Jesus. This revelation is so strong.

In Ephesians chapter two, the Bible says that in the ages to come, we'll still be getting a grip on the kindness of the Lord and what He did for us in Christ (Ephesians 2:7).

"*Therefore if any man be in Christ, he is a new creature* [or a new creation, or if any man be in Christ, let him *be* a new creature]..." (2 Corinthians 5:17, brackets TM). I'm going to do what Philemon said—I'm going to start acknowledging every good thing in me so that the communication of my faith may become effectual, and I can grow up into the full stature of the body of Christ. May you be the man or be the woman that God's called you to be in *full* measure! Hallelujah! Praise God! Let us walk in the perfection that's in Christ Jesus.

That word "new" Paul uses means "fresh." NEW!!! "Creature" means a new kind of being, a new species of being, not just overhauled. We've died with Christ, been buried with Christ and raised up with Christ. We're each a new creature in Christ—a God creature, a love creature, a faith creature, a Jesus creature. Praise God, we're seated with Him in heavenly places.

He went on to say, "*All things are become new*" (2 Corinthians 5:17). Look at verse eighteen, "*And all things are of God, who hath reconciled us to himself by Jesus Christ, and hath given to us the ministry of reconciliation.*"

He's saying these things God has made new are actually better than Adam had. We're in Christ. In Adam all died, in Christ we're made alive. "*God reconciled us to Himself, and God gave us a ministry of reconciliation; to witness that God was in Christ, reconciling the world unto Himself, not imputing their trespasses unto them; and hath committed unto us the word of reconciliation. Now then we are ambassadors for Christ, as though God did beseech you by us: we pray you in Christ's stead, be ye reconciled to God*" (verses 18-20, paraphrased).

Now get verse 21, "*For he hath made him* [God has made Jesus] *to be sin **for** us.*" There's that little preposition "for" or "on our behalf." He was made to be sin *for* us—substitution, as our substitute. He took our sin. He took our shame. He took our place. Praise God! He took our penalty. We've been raised with Him. Praise God! Hallelujah!

It wasn't just Jesus dying on the cross. Your old man was dying there with him. Galatians 2:20 tells us, "*I have been crucified with Christ...*" The Apostle Paul said, "*Nevertheless I live; yet not I, but Christ lives in me.*" That's a verse! I have been crucified with Christ. Nevertheless, I live. Yet not I, but Christ.

What? You mean the living Christ is living in me? I'm not just some empty shell going someplace doing nothing. In Christ, **I'm somebody going somewhere to do something fabulous for Jesus!** Christ lives in us.

Paul said, "*The life which I now live...I live by the faith of the Son of God, who loved me, and gave himself for me*" (Galatians 2:20). "*For he hath made him to be sin for us*" (2 Corinthians 5:21).

Christ not only took our sin—it doesn't just say He took our sin. It says He was *made to be sin*—not just the *acts* of sin, but the *condition* of sin. Jesus was not a sinner, but He was our substitute. He took our sin. He took our sin, took our condition and gave us a new position. What is it? Look what he said, "*That we might be made the righteousness of God in him*" (2 Corinthians 5:21).

Now, I want to challenge you to at least memorize those two Scriptures, 2 Corinthians 5:17 and 2 Corinthians 5:21. Write them down. Speak them out. Acknowledge them. Let it begin to work in you.

You might be saying, "I understand. I became a new creature."

Well, you understand in part, but remember, this thing keeps unfolding. It keeps going deeper. The work keeps penetrating our life—not only penetrating our life and pulsating in our lives, but radiating from our lives to a lost and dying world. I'm a new creature in Christ—a love creature, a God creature, a Jesus creature, a hope creature, a healthy creature, a rich creature. And I'm the righteousness of God in Christ because Jesus took my place.

THE RIGHTEOUSNESS OF GOD

That word, *righteousness*, is one we don't really use that much in the world. I think it's a very, very important word when we talk about righteousness. I am the *righteousness* of God in Christ. First of all, the word *righteousness* is a noun, which is a people, place, or thing. You are the righteousness of God. The word *righteous* is an adjective. So, we are righteous, but we are also the righteousness. God changed our condition! We became new creatures. We're not sinners; we're saints! *Bam*! We're not just forgiven; we're born again. We are made new. We're the righteousness of God.

That word *righteousness* means "innocent." It means "holy." It means "equitable." *Equitable* means "just and right." Well, righteousness means holy, equitable, and innocent. I like to say it means verified, bona fide, and reclassified!

I'm the righteousness of God. I have absolute right standing with the Father God based on the blood of Jesus. Hallelujah! He sees me in Christ. When I received Christ as my Lord and Savior, righteousness comes as a gift. **You can't get any more righteous than you are right now if you're a Christian. Righteousness is a gift.**

Now, we can grow in our *understanding* of righteousness like we can grow in new creation realities, but our *condition* has already been determined. We are the righteousness of God in Christ. I'm something different because of Jesus. I'm a new man because of Jesus. I'm a righteous new creature because of Jesus. I'm the righteousness of God in Christ Jesus. And so are you!

So when I begin to acknowledge these things, then the Bible says the communication of my faith become effectual. The Gospel is good news—that God would kill the old sin and raise a new man and call him righteousness! It put you and me into the family of God—sons and daughters of the living God! He restored our lives in every way! He called us His heirs and His joint-heirs with Jesus!

Righteousness is a term we must get used to. It really was the focus of the Apostle Paul's teaching. He taught about righteousness in Christ being a gift. He worked so hard as a Pharisee to be righteous in his own works, in his own labor. He said, "I was perfect in keeping the law" (Philippians 3:6, paraphrased). But when he came to Jesus, he realized that no man could be righteous on his own. Self-righteousness, the Bible says, is as filthy rags (Isaiah 64:6). But we have been made righteous through faith *in* Christ Jesus. Do you get it? **My union with Christ means I get the same stuff in me that He's got in Him.** So, that's the way it is. I'm the righteousness of God in Christ.

Believe the Gospel. It's good news! It may seem to be too good, but it's good news, and it's true! That Gospel is for you. They say the word "Gospel" is best defined as if someone comes from the battlefield and reports to the guys in the camp that the enemy has been defeated and the war is over; you can go home! Can you imagine the celebration? The victory is won!

Our victory is won in Christ. The battle is over. The devil is defeated. And Jesus is Lord! So we believe the Gospel. We trust the Gospel. We lean on God and the Gospel, and Jesus has made us His very own righteousness because of what He did.

What He has, we have. Who He is, we are. And this Scripture says we've been reconciled to God through Jesus Christ and His shed blood. Thank God for righteousness, which is a gift not based on works lest any man should boast (Ephesians 2:9).

GOD DOESN'T MAKE JUNK

In 2 Corinthians 5:18 he said this, "*And all things are of God.*" All of these things, these new creation things, come from God. God didn't give you junk. God doesn't make junk. He made you brand new. He made you righteous. Hallelujah! He made you His righteousness. Your sins are far removed. They've been remitted, for **God sees us in Christ.**

"*All things are of God, who hath reconciled us to himself by Jesus Christ, and hath given to us the ministry of reconciliation*" (2 Corinthians 5:18). So God reconciled us to Himself, and gave us a ministry of reconciliation. Now, think about that. The word "reconcile" means to make right, to settle issues.

Did you know new creation realities and the understanding of them can settle some issues in your life and family? Begin to acknowledge that you're a new creature in Christ. I'm a new creature in Christ Jesus, and I've been made the righteousness of God. That's who I am, and that's what I have. Acknowledge it. Say it. Dance about it. Sing about it. Believe it and receive it. Let it work for you. It'll begin to change some things and even settle some issues that you're facing in life. It also means to bring into harmony, to bring to peace, or to set at one again.

So Adam was separated from God by his sin. Jesus came and made us one—that's union. The little preposition *in* means *in* union. We're in Christ. Hallelujah! We are new creatures in Christ. We represent this new creation. And our job, it says here, is to operate in this ministry of reconciliation. We're not called to condemn people or even convince people. The Holy Spirit's job is to convince them of Christ. We, on the other hand, are called to live a new creation life in front of them. And when they see the Christ in us, they're going to want Him, and who He is, and what He can do.

SHOW AND TELL

We are also called to share this life with others. **I believe the Bible teaches that there are some things we're to show, and there are some things we're to tell. I like to call it "show and tell."** We tell some people; we show others. I found that for most cases, you've got to show your family; you've got to tell your friends. In order to show your family, you've got to live it in front of them. Get alone and get into the Word and pray; let the love of Christ radiate from you. Just show them that you're a new creature in Christ. Praise God! Let the communication of your faith become effectual (Philemon 1:6) as you acknowledge who you are in your private life with God, meditating on the "in Him" Scriptures. It begins to change how they see you because you're seeing yourself differently. You're seeing yourself in Christ, and Christ is coming out.

We're to live this life that Jesus called us to live. And it's a life He made ready for us to live. We don't have to figure it out; we just have to walk it out. The Bible says we walk by faith and not by sight. We are new creatures in Christ. We can act new, look new, and talk new because we "be" new. We've been reconciled to God. The Bible says, "*To wit* [witness], *that God was in Christ, reconciling the world unto himself, not imputing their trespasses unto them*" (brackets TM). In other words, God's not counting the sinner's mistakes. He's not counting up your mistakes either. He's forgiven them. The Bible says He cancels them in Christ. Praise God!

The sinner is already forgiven, but he's got to accept that forgiveness. That's the good news! He doesn't have to come and repent of all the sins he's done before he met Christ. When you get born again and you make a mistake, you can go to God and say, "I'm sorry." You can repent. But listen, the sinner can't remember all of his sins. His sins have been forgiven. So we're to tell him, "The table is spread! God's done something for you in Christ. Come and get it! He loves you! He's forgiven you! He wants you! He'll help you! There's hope in Jesus!"

CHRISTIANITY IS AN INSIDE JOB

Paul says, "*Not imputing their trespasses unto them; and hath committed unto us the word of reconciliation*" (verse 19). That phrase "committed unto us;" in the margin it says, "And has put *in us* the word of reconciliation." Christianity is an inside job.

When I raised my hands in that Chicago apartment room in 1970 and prayed for Jesus to come into my life, He changed me from the inside out. God has put something in you that will change your life and will help you deal with the issues that you face. It will also help you overcome every struggle! Others will begin to see your life—the love, the liberty that's in you because you are in Christ. The new creation realities are something that can be seen.

I'm in Christ. I'm a new creature. I'm in Christ. I'm the righteousness of God. I'm in Christ. I've been reconciled. I've been balanced. I've been set free. I've been made one together again with God. I don't know about you, but that gets me fired up! I've been made one together again with God in Christ Jesus.

The ministry of reconciliation restores us to divine favor. **God's not mad at you.** That's good news. God's not mad even at the sinner. He loves the sinner. He said in Isaiah, "Look, I'm not going to be mad at you." He released His anger on His Son at Calvary that God might shed His lovingkindness upon us.

This is the way God said it to me,

I'm not going down. God's not mad at me.
I'm not gonna drown. I have victory.
Weeping may endure for a night,
but joy, joy, joy, joy comes in the mornin' light.

When the Lord gave me that song, and I sang it out, *Joy comes in the mornin' light*, I heard the Holy Spirit go, "Whoop! Whoop!" (I didn't know the Holy Spirit could "whoop, whoop!" So when He said, "Whoop! Whoop!" He was getting into it.)

And that song is really a new creation reality song. I'm not going down! Why? Because I've been raised with Christ. God's not mad at me. Why? **Because He released His anger on His Son so that He could release His lovingkindness on me!** I'm not going down, and God's not mad at me. I'm not gonna drown. I have victory! How come? Because I'm victorious in Christ. Weeping may endure for a night. You're going to have some challenges in life. You're going to have some problems in life. But you have victory guaranteed in Christ Jesus.

So then I sang a little bit more. It went like this:

I'm stirring up some trouble for the devil. (Hope you are too.)
I'm not going down to his level. (Huh-uh)
I'm focused on the Lord. Great is my reward.
I'm free. I am free because
I'm not goin' down. God's not mad at me.
I'm not gonna drown. I have victory.
Weepin' may endure for a night,
but joy, joy, joy, joy comes in the morning light.

Thank God for new creation realities. Thank God we are new creatures in Christ. Begin to say it. Acknowledge it. Thank God we've been reconciled. It's been balanced. Jesus is Lord. He settled every issue. Issues that you face can be settled by new creation realities as you acknowledge who He is, what He's done, and who you are in Him. Peace will come. You're set at one again with God. You've got a victory guarantee!

HIS AMBASSADORS AND HIS EMBASSY

Psalm 100 says, "*We are His people, and the sheep of His pasture. Enter into his gates with thanksgiving, and into his courts with praise: be thankful unto him, and bless his name. For the Lord is good; his mercy is everlasting; and his truth endureth to all generations*" (verses 3-5).

You and I are in Christ. We are with Him, we are in Him, and we operate through Him because of what He did for us. God's not counting up our sins. He's canceled them. God doesn't see you as a sinner. He sees you as a son or a daughter, a saint, the righteousness of God in Jesus Christ. And He's given us a ministry. **All of us have this ministry to let this life come out of our lives so others can see the real Jesus stand up.**

He said in verse 20, "*Now then we are ambassadors for Christ*" (1 Corinthians 5:20). Well, that's really an "in Christ" reality even though it doesn't use the words "in Christ" in that verse. It says we are in Christ's stead, or in Christ's place endeavoring to reach others and let them know the Gospel—the good news that the war's over, the victory is ours.

He says we are ambassadors. What does an ambassador do? He represents another nation. We are ambassadors for Christ. In Him, through His grace, by His Word, through the help of the

Holy Spirit, we represent heaven. We represent Jesus. We are ambassadors for Christ!

The United States has ambassadors around the world, and the United States takes care of her ambassadors. God takes care of you and me. We represent Him. We're His ambassadors. And not only are we His ambassadors, but we are His embassy. What does that mean? An embassy is where the ambassador lives. Jesus lives *in* us! We house the very presence of God in our spirit. The Bible says our body has become the temple of the Holy Ghost.

As ambassadors, "*Now then we are ambassadors for Christ, and we are beseeching others to be reconciled to God*" (verse 20 paraphrased). We're calling out to them. We're reaching out to them. We're loving them. We're lifting them up. We're wanting them to know this real Jesus.

I like to say we are *compelling* others. The word *compelling* is a powerful word. Most of the time it's a very forceful word, but we're not forcing people to come to Christ. We're compelling them in a powerful, godly way. We're influencing them with love and life and liberty and joy, and we're showing them the real Jesus. We're letting John 3:16 become a reality that God's love has reached out to them, and is reaching out to them through us, that they may believe. "*Whosoever believeth in Him should not perish, but have everlasting life*" (John 3:16). John 3:16 is still a message calling for those to come to Christ.

We're called to call people to come to Christ, to live a life before them, to let them see that Jesus has spread the table. There's healing. There's help. There's peace. There's victory, and all they need to do is come because the Master is calling. As ambassadors, we represent Jesus. As His embassy, He lives in us. We're not going back. We're not going down. He's not mad at us. **We're going forward.** Hallelujah! His blood has been shed. His love is shed abroad in our hearts. We have been made the righteousness of God in Christ. That's who we are; that's what we have. We're on our way to something greater than we've ever known before. That's who I am. That's what I have. That's what Jesus made me to be. I walk in love. I live in Him. And I have victory. No doubt about it. Christ is king. I'm a new creation. I have a song to sing. That's who I am. That's what I have. That's what Jesus made me to be.

We read, "*Therefore if any man be in Christ, he is a new creature* [a new creation]" (2 Corinthians 5:17). A *creation* means original. He's a *new* creation without sin. Hallelujah! Praise God. We're the righteousness of God in Christ, new creatures.

I love that word *new*. You know, the New Testament is filled with the word *new*. We're new creatures in Christ. We've got a New Covenant. We drink new wine. We're to put on the new man. We've got a new name. Man, this thing gets better and better, doesn't it? We're called to invite people to let them see a living Christ in us. We petition them to come to Christ. We realize that we are His embassy. We are His ambassadors. We represent His love. We represent His life. We represent His legacy. We lift people. We love people because Jesus loves us.

The Jesus in us needs to stand up tall. Who He is and what He's done needs to be seen by the world. I believe the world is waiting and ready to see the real Jesus in you and me. And through new creation realities, we can certainly find ourselves in Him and be found in Him and others will see a living Christ in us. Jesus Christ is Lord to the glory of God the father. Hallelujah!

A CONFESSION SESSION

Now let's take a moment at the end of this chapter, and let's just have a little confession session. Let's just talk about some in Christ realities. I just want to show you several of my favorite ones. We've already quoted two, 2 Corinthians 5:17, and 2 Corinthians 5:21. But look at 1 Corinthians 1:30. It says this, "*But of Him are ye in Christ Jesus, who of God is made unto us wisdom, and righteousness, and sanctification, and redemption: That, according as it is written, He that glorieth* [rejoices or boasts], *let him glory* [rejoice, boast] *in the Lord*" (1 Corinthians 1:30-31, brackets TM). Hallelujah!

In other words, he said, "Get happy about being in Christ. Because in Christ is where all the answers are—in Christ." So this verse here says this, "*But of him are ye in Christ*" (1 Corinthians 1:30). So that means we are born of God, placed into Christ. So I would take this verse this way—I had it written on a 3x5 card—and I would say, "I am born of God, and I am in Christ Jesus. And God made Jesus unto me wisdom, and righteousness, and sanctification, and redemption. That's who I am. That's what I have." Praise God! I have wisdom. I have righteousness. I have sanctification. I have redemption. That's who I am. That's what I have. And I would just start rejoicing in the fact that I have wisdom, and righteousness, and sanctification, and redemption.

Now, that doesn't mean I know everything or even know everything I need to know, but that means I have total access in Christ to anything I will ever need. Of Him, in Christ, I have wisdom, righteousness, sanctification, and redemption. Hallelujah! That's who I am. That's what I have.

Let's look at another one. Look at Romans 8:1, which we'll come back to later in the book: "*There is therefore now no condemnation to them which are in Christ Jesus.*" No guilt, no sense of wrong, no failure complex. Praise God, it's gone like yesterday. Gone like the devil when Jesus blew him away. Hallelujah!

"*There is therefore now no condemnation to them which are in Christ Jesus*" (Romans 8:1). That's me. That's you. No condemnation to them which are in Christ Jesus, who walk not after the flesh, but after the Spirit. We're not going after the flesh to try to receive our righteousness. We receive from the Holy Spirit. We receive from God by faith. This gift of righteousness has no condemnation, no guilt, no shame. Why? Verse two, "*For the law of the Spirit of life in Christ hath made me free from the law of sin and death.*" That's who I am! That's what I have!

What did Brother Hagin say to do? He said to declare that's who I am and that's what I have. The law of the Spirit of life in Christ Jesus has made me free from the law of sin and death (Romans 8:2). I'm no longer bound by the enemy. I'm set free by the blood of Jesus. I love that verse, "*The law of the Spirit of life in Christ....*" Where is the Spirit of life? It's in Christ. These are in Christ realities, new creation realities, in Him, in whom, in Christ. Hallelujah! Thank you, Jesus. He has set us free! I'm free from sin. I'm free from Satan's dominion. I'm free in Christ Jesus.

So you take a verse like that, and you just begin to acknowledge "That's who I am. That's what I have. That's who Jesus made me to be. I walk in love. I live in Him, and I have victory." No doubt about it; Jesus Christ is King. I am a new creation. I have a song to sing. That's who I am. That's what I have. That's what Jesus made me to be.

Well, let's look at another one. Go to 2 Corinthians 2:14, "*Now thanks be unto God, which always causeth us to triumph in Christ.*" Where? In Christ. My victory is in Christ. The new creation is victorious. Jesus is victorious. He arose from the dead. Praise God! He whipped the devil, stripped the devil, defeated the devil, and rose out of there victorious. And His victory is my victory. So it says, "*Now, thanks be unto God, which always causeth us to triumph in Christ.*" So we have victory. Praise the Lord! Hallelujah! Thank you, Jesus. Amen. I have victory in Christ.

Now, watch: "*And* [he] *maketh manifest the savour of his knowledge by us in every place. For we are the fragrance of Christ* [one translation says]" (2 Corinthians 2:14-15 paraphrased).

So I have a song that says:

Don't smell like defeat. Smell like de-head.
You've been raised with Christ. You're not dead.
Lift your hands and rejoice. Lift up your voice.
He has made you complete. In Jesus Christ there's victory.
So don't smell like defeat. Don't smell like defeat!
Smell like de-head. [Who's the head? Jesus.]
We've been raised with Christ. [Think about it.]
We're not dead [New life. New creation.]
Lift your hands and rejoice. Lift up your voice.
He has made you complete. In Jesus Christ there's victory.
So don't smell like defeat.

So this verse here, I just take and say, "Thanks be unto God who always causes me to triumph in Christ. That's who I am. That's what I have."

Always remember, you're not just fighting *for* victory; you're fighting *from* victory. My dear friend, Mark Hankins, made that statement. We're not fighting *for* victory. We're fighting *from* a position of victory. We are victorious. You are victorious in Christ right now. Even in the midst of the problem, you are victorious. So begin to acknowledge that. Philemon says acknowledge every good thing that's in you in Christ. This is a good thing. I'm in Christ, and

God always gives me the victory. And all you've got to do is say, "Devil, get under my feet! Jesus has given me the victory!"

Happy new you! The old you was dead in your sins; the new you is the righteousness of God in Christ Jesus!

CHAPTER 3:

WHO DO YOU SEE?

Remember in our last chapter we talked about we are ambassadors for Christ. We represent Jesus, and He lives in us. So, in Christ means that He's in us, and we're in Him. And actually, we're not just His representation on earth, but He's representing us in heaven as well. The Bible said He's ever interceding for us. So there's a heaven-earth connection going on in us because of who we are in Christ.

We learned we're not only ambassadors, but we are His embassy. Christ lives in us through the Holy Spirit and by His Word. The real Jesus will stand up on the inside of anyone who will come to understand and begin to understand the new creation realities that we have in Christ Jesus.

SEE JESUS

The Bible said there were certain Greeks that came to Philip and said, "*Philip, we would like to see Jesus*" (John 12:20-21 paraphrased). And I think of that verse often. I believe people are still saying today, "We want to see Jesus. We want to see Jesus in the Church." And that's what this is. This new creation reality is about a living Christ Who is living in us and letting people see the real Jesus in the earth today—His love, and the life, and the liberty that only Christ can bring. There's no hope anywhere else except in Jesus.

We used to sing that old song years ago that said,

> *"Only Jesus can satisfy your soul.*
> *Only He can change a heart and make it whole.*
> *He'll give you peace you never knew, sweet love, and joy, and heaven too.*
> *'Cuz only Jesus can satisfy your soul."*

We know that. We've come to Jesus. You're reading this book because you love Jesus. You want to know more about His Word, about His plan, and about His purpose for your life. And learning "in Christ" realities will cause that to come to pass because that is really who we are. And that is really what we have. That's exactly what Jesus paid for.

So I like to say, "Will the real Jesus please stand up?" Stand up in us because of who we are in Him! Did you know this? The more we come to know these "in Christ" realities, these new creation realities, the more Jesus is seen in our life. The more we see Him, the more others see Him in us.

In this chapter, we're going to ask, "Who do you see?" I found out it's not just *what* you see but *who* do you see. Because *who* you see will affect *what* you see, and many times will affect *how* you see. We want to see Jesus. We want to see ourselves in Him. We are new creatures in Christ Jesus. Old things have passed away. All things have become new. That's who I am. That's what I have.

I see myself in Him. I see myself reconciled to Him. Hallelujah! Nothing missing, nothing broken. I see myself in harmony with God. I see myself with a ministry of His goodness to others, letting them know that they are forgiven, that Christ has a plan for their life. Letting them know that nothing is too hard, no valley is too low, no problem is too big for Jesus Christ.

Who do you see?

THEY'LL SEE JESUS IN YOU

We're going to look at 2 Corinthians 3:2, where it says, "*Ye are our epistle written in our hearts, known and read of all men.*" He said, "Somebody's watching you. Somebody's reading you. Somebody needs to see Jesus in you." That's what "in Christ" realities, new creation realities, are all about—letting the new creation that God accomplished in Christ live big in us so that the world can see a living, loving Jesus. Only He can satisfy our soul. Hallelujah! Thank you, Jesus.

Look at verse three, "*Forasmuch as ye are manifestly declared to be the epistle of Christ ministered by us....*" That's pretty heavy. We are examples of Christ and His love. That's what God did. We can't do that. We simply acknowledge it, and it becomes effective as we acknowledge it. Hallelujah! He made us to be something in Him. We acknowledge that. We acknowledge His righteousness. We acknowledge the new creation. We acknowledge His favor and His grace. And He causes it to emanate from us, and people can see a living Christ in us.

He said, "*You are the epistle of Christ ministered by us, written not with ink, but with the Spirit of the living God; not in tables of stone, but in fleshy tables of the heart*" (2 Corinthians 3:2-3, paraphrased).

Listen, Christianity is an inside job. God did something on the inside of us. He made us new creatures in Christ Jesus. Righteousness is a spiritual force on the inside of us.

Religion tries to change people from the outside. Christianity does it from the inside. Jesus is not religious. Jesus is *relational.* Remember those little prepositions; one of the first things I taught you was that a preposition is that little word in front of a noun or pronoun that magnifies or expresses relationship. I'm *in* Christ. I was crucified *with* Christ. I was buried *with* Christ. I'm raised, seated *with* Christ. He did it *for* me. Now *through* Him, I can live this dynamic new creation lifestyle. Hallelujah! Amen.

Verse four, "*And such trust have we through Christ to God-ward.*" What God did in Christ is the real deal. "*Not that we are sufficient of ourselves to think anything as of ourselves; but our sufficiency is of God*" (verse 5) Hallelujah!

Then Paul went on to say, "*God has made us able ministers of the New Testament; not of the letter, but of the spirit: for the letter killeth, but the spirit giveth life*" (verse 6).

Now, one translation said it this way—and this is what I want to point out in this verse right here—that God has made us *dispensers* of the New Testament, this new creation. We are living this life. We are dispensing this life wherever we go. We are acknowledging, according to Philemon verse six, every good thing in us in Christ. And it's growing in us. It's working in us.

Christ became our substitute. Christ did what He did for us so we could be united with Him in His life, in His victory, in His power, in His grace. And the same stuff that's in Him is in us. I got some God-stuff in me. I've got some Jesus-stuff in me. I'm a God man. I'm a Jesus man. I'm a love man. Hallelujah! And so are you! Jesus made it that way.

We acknowledge the fact that Christ in us, the hope of glory, is the heart of the New Testament. And with the New Testament working in us and through us, others can see a new living Jesus—in us. We are dispensers of the New Testament. We're peddling something around town. We're living a life that shows the grace of God, the goodness of God, the glory of God, the power of God. Hallelujah! And as we live this life, *whoa*! Something great takes place. Something good happens, not only to us, but happens *through* us. Glory to God!

Look at 2 Corinthians 3:7, "*But if the ministration of death, written and engraven in stones, was glorious, so that the children of Israel could not stedfastly behold the face of Moses for the glory of his countenance; which glory was to be done away: How shall not the ministration of the spirit be rather glorious?*"

Do you remember the Old Testament story where Moses went on the mountain and visited with God? He came down, and his face was shining. Paul is saying, "That's nothing compared to what's in you and in me." **In this New Covenant, that very glory of God on the face of Moses has actually shone in our heart through Jesus—and greater than Moses!** And the New Covenant is more glorious than the Old Covenant. What we got from Jesus is better than what Moses got.

Thank God for Moses on the mountain, but it's not about what Moses did on the mountain. It's about what *Jesus* did on the mountain! What Jesus did on the mountain outshines everything. The cross and the power of that cross, and the power of that empty tomb, and that power in that upper room is greater! Glory to God!

We identify with that. We've got identity with God! We've got what Jesus had! Christ in us the hope of glory!

STAY IN THE NEW

Paul goes on to say, "*That ministry in the Old Covenant was a ministry of condemnation, much more doth the ministration of righteousness exceed in glory*" (2 Corinthians 3:9 paraphrased).

Did you know that no man could keep the law? You know, the law was to point out our inability to be righteous in our own strength. Jesus came, and in Him, we've become the righteousness of God. Hallelujah! Praise God. God gave it to us as a *gift*. Think about that. And He said this righteousness exceeds in glory. So he's saying that there's no comparison between the old and the new.

Listen, a lot of people want to go back under the Old Covenant. You don't have to go back under the Old Covenant. We're to live in the New Covenant, in the righteousness that Jesus provided. It's a gift from God. We are the righteousness of God in Christ Jesus, and it's glorious. Hallelujah! Glory to God.

So we're to get our eyes on Jesus—who He is and what He's done. It is so awesome that this one Man, Jesus Christ, could be God's choice and man's best to cut covenant for you and me and that we get in on His deal. We are in Him, made full and have come to fullness of life. In Christ, we too, are filled with the Godhead—the Father, the Son, and the Holy Ghost.

I love the verse that says that. It's one of my favorite "in Him" Scriptures—Colossians 2:9-10 in the Amplified version. We are in Him made full and have come to fullness of life. In Christ we too are filled with the Godhead—the Father, Son, and the Holy Ghost—and reach full spiritual stature. I sing a song about that. It goes like this:

I am in Him.

The Lord Jesus Christ made full and have come to fullness of life.

I am a new creature created in Christ by my Father God.

And I too am filled with the Godhead—Father, Son, and Holy Ghost.

I too am filled with the Godhead—Father, Son, and Holy Ghost.

I am in Him. The Lord Jesus Christ made full and have come to fullness of life.

I am a new creature created in Christ by my Father God.

Hallelujah!

I used to sing those songs a lot and still do because they are "in Christ" realities. They are new creation realities. We are in Him made full and have come to fullness of life. And the life that's in Him is a glorious life. It's greater than the glory of the Old Testament. We've got the glory of the New Testament in the Son of God. What He has, we have. What He did, He did for us on our behalf. We died with Him. We're raised with Him. We're seated with Him. We're living in Him and through Him we function. Praise the Lord! Hallelujah!

YOU'VE BEEN UPGRADED

What Jesus did is better than any glory of the Old Testament. That's what this chapter's about. I wanted us not to simply take these verses, although we could have just taken "in Him," "in Christ," "in whom" verses. But I wanted us to see the whole context of the Apostle Paul's teaching. He spent lots of time talking about the difference between the old and the new, talking about righteousness as a gift and who we are in Christ. He's saying the old had no glory at all compared to the new. It's not even a comparison!

He said in 2 Corinthians 3:11, "*For if that which is done away was glorious, much more that which remaineth is glorious.*" The old that was done away with was glorious; now this one will never be replaced. Did you know the New Testament will never need an upgrade? Don't you get tired of upgrades sometimes? Upgrade this, upgrade that. Listen, the New Testament will never need an upgrade! One Man did the deal for all men for all time; He made the sacrifice that was enough and sufficient for all of us for all time. Hallelujah! Glory to God! And we are in Him! I'm in Him. I'm in Him made full. You're made full. Full of what? Full of God things. Full of good things. Full of hope. Full of faith. Full of joy. Full of healing. Praise God, I'm made full in Christ! Christ did it for me. He was my substitute. I died with Him. I'm raised with Him. Now I'm in Him! And through Him I function. In Him I live and move and have my being! Praise God!

So this new deal that God cut called the New Covenant, He made a covenant with His Son, Jesus as our substitute so we have covenant as well. He is the real deal—never to be replaced, never to be updated. It is more glorious than anything that happened in the Old Covenant.

Verse 12, "*Seeing then that we have such hope, we use great plainness of speech.*" Paul goes on, "*And not as Moses, which put a veil over his face, that the children of Israel could not stedfastly look to the end of that which is abolished: But their minds were blinded: for until this day remaineth the same vail untaken away in the reading of the old testament; which vail is done away in Christ*" (2 Corinthians 3:13-14 KJV).

Praise God! The veil is done away in Christ. See that little "in Christ?" God has opened up all of heaven to us through Christ. Everything that He has is ours. The Bible says we are joint heirs with Him, heirs of God and joint-heirs with Christ (see Romans

8:17). The light of the glorious Gospel has shined upon us. That light comes to us as we acknowledge every good thing that's in us in Christ Jesus (see Philemon 1:6). The Bible said that God will light our candle (see Psalm 18:28). And by our God we can run through a troop, and leap over every wall (see Psalm 18:29).

LIGHT IT UP

So when we come to Christ, we get lit. Hallelujah! It's an open revelation of His goodness and His love and His mercy and His grace. We receive everything He has for us. It's not hidden *from* us. It's hidden *for* us. And in Christ, it belongs to us. Hallelujah! Glory to God!

We accept this fact that Jesus Christ is Lord. And in Him we can see clearly who God is, what God did, who Christ is, what Christ did, and how it affects us. We can see this truth that in Him we live, in Him we move, and in Him we have our being. We are made full by His grace, full by His power, full by His sacrifice. Hallelujah! Nothing's hidden! Openness! All of God is ours!

All of God's plan and purpose will come to pass in Christ Jesus. We are His people and the sheep of His pasture. The veil is done away in Christ, meaning we can look right into the very glory of God. We can look right into the very plan of God in Christ. We can look and see who Jesus is, what Jesus did. We can see Him as He is. And we can know that is the way we are in Him.

The more we see what God did in Christ, the more we light up with His love, the more we light up with His life. The more we acknowledge who we are in Christ—take those little verses, about 130 of them—and begin to acknowledge that's who you are, what you have. The more we light up, the more light comes. We light up in Christ.

Psalm 18:28-29 says this, "*For thou wilt light my candle: the Lord my God will enlighten my darkness. For by thee I have run through a troop; and by my God have I leaped over a wall.*"

The veil has been done away with. The light of God has come to us. And the more we see what Christ did for us and the more the light comes to us, we can see more clearly. When the veil is done away, we can see clearly who Christ is and what Christ did.

Proverbs 20:27 says, "*The spirit of man is the candle of the Lord.*" When the Lord lights my candle, He lights up my spirit with insight and revelation and salvation and hope so that I can see clearly who He is and what He's done for me. My candle gets lit, and the Lord enlightens my darkness. And when I'm lit with the revelation of who I am in Christ, when I get lit with new creation realities, the Bible said I can run through a troop, and I can leap over every wall! Praise God! Hallelujah! Glory to God! Amen!

You're about to leap over circumstances. You're about to leap over situations. You're about to leap through that thing that's trying to hold you back. You're a new creature in Christ; old things have passed away; all things have become new (see 2 Corinthians 5:17). You're the righteousness of God in Christ Jesus (see 1 Corinthians 1:30). You are a letter from God read of all men, and the Spirit of God is working in you and me today helping us to see plainly who Jesus is and what Jesus did.

And when we get that view, I'm telling you, we can run through the troop and leap over the wall. I like to say you can't leap if you ain't lit. So, get lit!

You might say, "Well, how do I get lit?" By understanding and living new creation realities.

PUT IT ALL TOGETHER

I wanted to read some of these things together so we can see the context of what Paul is saying. The veil is done away. The light comes. You get lit, you can run through a troop. Knowing who you are in Christ, you can leap over any wall. These realities are important.

Going on, 2 Corinthians 3:15-16 says, "*But even unto this day, when Moses is read, the vail is upon their heart. Nevertheless when it shall turn to the Lord, the vail shall be taken away.*" Praise God! Just turn to the Lord, and the light will come.

When I was in that little, old apartment in Chicago in 1970, I just turned to the Lord. I cried out to the Lord. And man, the moment my heart turned to Him, the light of God hit that place. The love of God filled that place. And both my wife and I were born again and filled with Christ life. Praise the Lord!

God's not holding anything back. He's just waiting for us to come get it. He's just waiting for us to drink. And that's what you're doing in this book. You're learning who you are in Christ, the realities of the new creation, what Jesus did, and how it affects who you are and how you live.

Verse 17, "*Now the Lord is that Spirit: and where the Spirit of the Lord is, there is liberty.*" Hallelujah! God has not called us to bondage. He's not called us to religion. He's called us to freedom—freedom in Christ Jesus. We're free to be all He's called us to be. Not to be held down by the hands of man, or the dictates of the past, or by the world's system, or by the devil, but to be set free in the glorious liberty as sons and daughters of the living God in Christ. Praise God! I said I'm in Christ, made full and have come to fullness of life.

So he said there's liberty. Now watch verse 18; it's what I want to get to, "*With open face, beholding as in a glass the glory of the Lord, are changed into the same image from glory to glory, even as by the Spirit of the Lord*" (2 Corinthians 3:18).

Boy, that said a mouthful, didn't it? It says when we look into the Word, the Word of God becomes like a mirror. When we look into the Word of God, we look into "in Christ" realities, it's like a mirror. We see the glory of the Lord. And as we look at that and acknowledge that, it says we are changed into that same image. Hallelujah! It says there's a changing going on in us; as we look into the Word, who we are in Christ, and we begin to acknowledge who we are in Christ, the Holy Spirit begins to change us into that image. So in reality, when we look in the Word, we don't just see Jesus, we see ourselves. We see ourselves in Him. When we see ourselves in Him and begin to acknowledge who we are in Him, everything begins to change.

I can't change myself. God changed me for me, but I have to let it be. I acknowledge it, and it starts working in me—working on issues, working on problems, taking me deeper, until the very image of the resurrected Messiah is seen in full force in the Church. Wouldn't that be something? That's the real Jesus that needs to stand up in the Church today. Let Him be seen. Let it be said we are those people that believe who He says we are. We are those people who believe we can do what He says we can do. We are those people who believe we have what He says we have. We look into the Word, we see who we are in Christ, and the Holy Spirit goes to work as we acknowledge that by faith—that's who I am, that's what I have—He goes to work transforming us and our situations and causing them to line up with the resurrected Savior.

Who do you see? Well, I see Jesus. That's who I see. Who else do you see? I see me. I look like Him, and so do you!

I look like my earthly Daddy. I can't help myself. Do you know why? Because he's in me, and I was in him. I've got some of his traits.

You and I look like Jesus. He's in you; you're in Him. So I see me when I look into the Word. Who do you see? I see me in Him. I see Him in me.

I have a song that goes:

I in Him, and He in me.

We in them, and they in we.

What a glorious place to be, hid with Christ in God.

Because I'm dead to the world,

and my life is hid with Christ in God my Father, Hallelujah!

So we see Him in us the hope of glory. We experience freedom and liberty. One translation said, "unrestrained access." God is not withholding anything from us in Christ. It all belongs to us. We are heirs of God and joint heirs with Jesus. That means we have what He has. We get what He got. But it has to be acknowledged. It has to be received. We have to let it be. Let it be! Let it work. And through that acknowledgment—that's who I am, that's what I have—then I start functioning with unrestrained access. We have security clearance in Christ. What happens in Christ is not above your pay grade. There is nothing the Lord will hold back from us. When we dive into this image of who Christ is in us, we begin to see the way things really are—*I in Him; He in me; we in them; they in we. What a glorious place to be, hid with Christ in God.*

AN X-RAY OF REDEMPTION

Through this, we begin to see not just a photo of redemption but an X-ray of redemption. It shows what's going on inside the mind of God and the plan of God. Praise God, we see Him, who He is, and what He's done.

Mark Hankins said something like this, "The Gospel is a photo of redemption. We see Christ on the cross, a photo. But Paul's letters are an X-ray. We see what was going on inside Christ on the Cross."

We see that we were there with Him, that we died with Him, that God had a plan that set us free and raised us up to sit with Him in heavenly places. I'm in charge in Christ. I'm not over Christ, or over God, or bossing God around. But we have been given *authority*. We have been given dominion, and we're in charge. We can tell the enemy, "Back off! Bow your knee in Jesus' name! Hallelujah!" We can take our place as citizens of heaven and sons and daughters of the living God in Christ. Praise God! Give the enemy no place. Look upon Jesus and all of His glory and all of His majesty and realize He is the Greater One, and His Spirit is in us. And the Greater One resides in us to put us over. We are victorious in Christ.

Second Corinthians 2:14, "*Now thanks be unto God, which always causeth us to triumph in Christ.*" Praise God! Hallelujah! We have been given the victory. The very image of Christ is in us today. The very glory of God is in us. The very love of God is shed abroad in our heart. We see ourselves in Him.

We see the reflection of the mirror, and it looks like Him because it *is* Him. It's Christ *in* us the hope of glory. It's us in Him, and He in us. And we're here to carry out His plan. As we look at

Him, in whom, in Christ, we see ourselves and we are changed and transformed by the Spirit of the living God.

The world needs to see us in Christ. The world needs to see you and me living that life that God intended us to live. I believe a key to walking in victory is realizing that He's in me, the hope of glory. And that image is becoming clearer and clearer every day. It'll get so big, it'll just overwhelm the works of the enemy. And life is filled with love, joy, peace, provision, power, and victory. Praise God! Hallelujah!

Let's read verse 18 again, "*But we all, with open face beholding as in a glass* [mirror] *the glory of the Lord, are changed into the same image from glory to glory, even as by the Spirit of the Lord*" (2 Corinthians 3:18, brackets TM).

So, it doesn't all come at one time. Although the work is done, we grow into it. Like the Apostle Paul said, "I'm still going deeper. I'm still going deeper in who I am in Christ. My high calling is in Christ." Your high calling is in Christ, and we're going deeper.

So, let's go to the fourth chapter and watch this. "*Therefore,*" he said, "*seeing we have this ministry, as we have received mercy, we faint not*" (2 Corinthians 4:1, paraphrased). He said, "In this ministry of the New Testament, teaching people who they are in Christ," he said, "we have renounced hidden things of dishonesty, and craftiness, and all that." He said, "We're representing Jesus. We're not looking for any kind of gimmick. We're looking to the power of the Word of God, the Holy Spirit, to work in us that which is right. And we're going deeper than we've ever been before" (2 Corinthians 4:2, paraphrased).

Then he goes on to say, "Look if the Gospel is hid, it is hid to them that are lost. It's not hid from us" (2 Corinthians 4:3, paraphrased) The good news is, Jesus won the war. The devil is defeated. Jesus is Lord. Victory is ours. Hallelujah! Glory to God! Hallelujah!

Verse four, "*In whom the god of this world hath blinded the minds of them which believed not, lest the light of the glorious Gospel of Christ, who is the image of God, should shine unto them.*"

The devil is trying to blind people from this reality, so they don't know what God did in Christ and what that means. So in a book like this, we take time to learn about it, look at Scripture about it, and then we begin to acknowledge who we are in Christ. It changes everything. The light of the glorious Gospel begins to shine in us, on us, and through us in a new and living way. When we begin to declare, "That's who I am. That's what I have in Christ. Hallelujah! I'm who God says I am. I can do what God says I can do. I have what God says I have. No weapon formed against me shall prosper. The devil is under my feet. Jesus is Lord. I'm a new creature in Christ Jesus. I'm made full in God. I have the victory."

Keep moving toward God like never before. Keep moving toward who He called us to be. We're moving toward the new creation realities and revelation in the righteousness of God and the plan of God. We're moving toward the river of God's great provision.

Don't let any enemy come in, deceive you, hold you back, and trick you trying to get you out of God's plan. The Gospel is enough. The Gospel is powerful. Christ took our place so that we could become as He is in this world.

It says in 1 John 4:17, "*As he is, so are we in this world.*" Isn't that something? So we can see right there, God's intention was not just one Man dying on the cross, but was a new creation being born. Not just a new person, but generation after generation of a new creation.

God had a plan, and, boy, did it surprise the devil! The devil thought he was getting rid of Jesus. He didn't know that he was working in God's plan by crucifying Jesus or that he was actually planting Jesus and a crop of new believers was coming up. And we've been getting a harvest every year! People getting saved and set free! Praise God!

GET EXCITED

It's okay to get excited about this stuff!

I was preaching down in Tucson several years ago, and right in the middle of worship a big old guy goes, "YEEEEEH!" It was loud. I looked around, and it was a guy about 6'5". And I don't know, he weighed maybe 230 or 240. He was so excited. So I asked the pastor about it after the service. I said, "Tell me about that guy."

He said, "Well, he showed up at church one day, and he did that during the praise and worship, got so excited!" He went on, "Some of my people came to me and said, 'What are you going to do about that, Pastor, next week if he shows up?' I looked at him and said, 'Well, I was thinking about asking him to sit on the front row, so he'd show us how we ought to worship God because it was real. He wasn't just doing it for a show. I mean, it was just coming out of his heart.'"

I said, "What's his story?"

The pastor said, "Well, he got left for dead, basically, in an accident of some sort. And there was just no way he was going to live. But God brought him through. God saved him. God raised him up. And ever since, he's been so excited! He gets in church and gets in the presence of God, and he just goes, 'Yeaaaah!'"

This man realized what God had done for him, and we need to be more like that.

So, some places I go I have people stand up and say, "Everybody go, *Yeeaaahhh*!" I think sometimes we ought to get more excited about what Jesus did for us. As He is, so are we in this world—*Yeeeaah*! That will make you shout if you think about it! That's a good deal. We are new creatures in Christ! *Yeeeaaah*! We're the righteousness of God. Just expressing our gratitude to a loving God who sent His Son to set us free should inspire us to praise. There was no other way to be set free. It is not going to happen. You can't get free from Satan's dominion unless you know Jesus. In Adam all die; in Christ all are made alive. You're either in one or the other. And if you're in Christ, you ought to be going, "***Yeeeeaah***!" Hallelujah!

LIVE LIFE ON THE VICTORY SIDE

I'm so excited about what Jesus did. "*As he is, so are we in this world*" (1 John 4:17). And that's the message Paul was preaching in 2 Corinthians chapters three and four. He said there's an image God wants you to see. And that image is an image of Christ *in you*—and you in Him. As you see it and say it, then the Holy Spirit transforms you in it, and it begins, not only to affect you, but everything and everyone around you. Lives begin to change. Jesus is glorified and great things happen.

Look at 2 Corinthians 4:4, "*In whom the god of this world hath blinded the minds of them which believe not, lest the light of the glorious gospel of Christ, who is the image of God, should shine unto them.*"

That's what happens to you and I when we come to Jesus. The light of the glorious Gospel shines in our hearts, the very image of Christ Himself.

What's your part? Let it be. Oh, Jesus, let it be. Let it be in me. Let it be in us, I pray!

Let's read a couple of more verses. We read in 2 Corinthians 4:5-6, "*For we preach not ourselves, but Christ Jesus the Lord; and ourselves your servants for Jesus' sake. For God, who commanded the light to shine out of darkness, hath shined in our hearts, to give the light of the knowledge of the glory of God in the face of Jesus Christ.*"

He said, "If you think Moses had a light on his face, wait till you see the light Jesus has on His face!" And the light that's on His face is the same light that's shining in our hearts. What He is, we are. And what He got, we get. We are in Him, and He's in us. This is the Gospel! It's Christ in us, the hope of glory. He set us free. He set us free by His love. Thank you, Jesus! Hallelujah!

Look at verses 7-9, "*But we have this treasure in earthen vessels, that the excellency of the power may be of God, [it is not of us, but of God Himself]. We may be troubled on every side, but not distressed; we may be perplexed, but not in despair. We may be persecuted, but not forsaken. We may be cast down, but not destroyed*" (paraphrased).

We may be knocked down, but never knocked out. We may be thrown down, but never broken. We always rise up in victory because of what Christ did for us. The life of Christ is being manifest in our bodies because we are *in* Him, and He is *in* us!

Praise God! We are to live life on the victory side. You can step over from the problem side onto the victory side because Jesus gives us the victory in Christ. God always causes us to triumph in

Christ, and through Him, He gives us the victory! Hallelujah! Praise God! I am victorious in Christ. Say it out loud to yourself: "I am victorious in Christ." It's okay to get excited about it! Shout it from the rooftops!

CHAPTER 4:

PERFECT IN CHRIST

I had this song in my heart as I started this chapter. It's pretty simple. It goes like this:

Be glorified. Be glorified. Be glorified. Be glorified.
Be glorified in the heavens. Be glorified in the earth.
Be glorified in this temple. Jesus, Jesus, be Thou glorified.

I love that when it talks about "glorified in the heavens, in the earth, and in this *temple*." The Bible says that our bodies have become the temple of the Holy Spirit, which, by the way, is a new creation reality. That couldn't happen before. In the Old Testament, the Spirit of God was upon the priest, the king, or the prophet. In the New Testament, guess what happened? Jesus cleansed us by His blood. He prepared us to be a temple of God, a habitation of the Spirit of God.

I want to read one of our theme Scriptures for this entire book. Philemon only has one chapter, and verse number six says this: "*That the communication of thy faith may become effectual by the acknowledging of every good thing which is in you in Christ Jesus.*"

Well, that little phrase, "in Christ Jesus," signals to us that this is a new creation reality Scripture. God does good things. And He's a good God. And He's done good things *in us in Christ*. So, if we will acknowledge those good things that He did in us in Christ, by Christ, then our faith becomes more effectual, more energized, sets us apart, and is easily seen by others. Praise God.

When we acknowledge who we are in Christ, we're actually glorifying the Lord. Listen, that's what Jesus did for us. When we say we are the righteousness of God in Christ, we're bragging on Jesus. When we acknowledge who He is and what He did and what He made us to be, that is glorifying Jesus. And when we glorify Jesus and magnify Jesus, it just seems like He becomes bigger in our life, in our heart, and in our mind. His redemptive work, His precious blood, and all that He paid for grow in our vision.

We are in the process of being conformed to the image of Christ. Remember the chapter we just read, *Who Do You See?* Jesus is in you in the mirror. And we are conformed, or the Bible says we are changed, into that image that we see. So when we see who we are in Christ and acknowledge that, we're glorifying the Lord because it depends on Him. And at the same time, we're being transformed into that very same image. This makes our faith effectual.

The mystery of the Gospel is not only what God did in Christ, but also what God did in you and me in Christ, and what He's still doing today. He didn't leave the work at Calvary. Thank God! Calvary meant something, but He didn't stop there. He didn't leave it at an empty tomb. He didn't even leave it in the upper room.

It says on the day of Pentecost when they were in one accord, in one place, in Acts chapter two, that they were all baptized with the Holy Spirit and with fire. That's one of the ministries that Jesus came to do. (And, by the way, being baptized in the Holy Spirit, being born of the Spirit is an in Christ reality.)

God literally got out of the box. He was in that box, the Ark of the Covenant. The presence of God dwelt there. But when Jesus came and the veil of the temple was torn from top to bottom, God got out of that box and moved into our hearts. That is a new creation reality! Praise God! Hallelujah! Thank you, Jesus! Amen!

I believe that a Spirit-filled lifestyle is part of the new creation that we are to live in. And when God got out of that box and they came out of that upper room, the Bible says 3,000 souls were saved in one day. That's pretty powerful, isn't it?

Listen, we haven't seen nothing yet—not only what God is capable of doing in us or through us, but what He plans on doing in the earth in these days. And you and I taking time to study these new creation realities will enable us to go deeper than we've ever gone before in fulfilling the plan and purpose of God in our lives.

THE HIDDEN COMES TO LIGHT

In light of Philemon, which is a theme Scripture through the whole series, let's look at Colossians 1:25: "*Whereof I am made a minister, according to the dispensation of God which is given to me for you, to fulfil the word of God.*" Verse 26, "*Even the mystery which hath been hid from ages and from generations, but now is made manifest to his saints.*"

Do you realize that we are living in that period of time when things that were hidden in God from the beginning of time have come to light? That is this new creation reality. This is what God had in mind; something that could not be stolen, like Adam's dominion was stolen in the beginning—something that could not be improved upon, something that was purchased and ratified by the precious blood of Jesus Christ, the Lamb of God. Hallelujah! And He said to us it's been revealed in the now. Verse 27 tells us, "*To whom God would make known what is the riches of the glory of this mystery among the Gentiles, which is Christ in you, the hope of glory.*"

I start getting excited just thinking about this! Christ in you and me? You and I in Christ? That's a double whammy for the devil! He can't handle you. He can't handle this revelation. This new creation is powerful. It is God designed, and it is God's plan for our generation and for this time.

Paul said that this mystery was hidden but now is revealed. And then he said this is the mystery that Christ would take up residence in our heart, and we would find ourselves in Him. Remember the Apostle Paul, after thirty years in ministry, said that he finds himself in Christ. He was still looking. He was still listening. He was still searching. He was still going deeper than he'd ever been before after decades.

This Scripture says to us the mission and the ministry of the Apostle Paul was to reveal this mystery to the Church—that now Christ is in us and we are in Him. I love it when it said, "*The riches of the glory of this mystery is Christ in you*" (Colossians 1:27, paraphrased). It's like he said, "It don't get any better than that." God's not just far out, far off, somewhere, sometime. He's *here* right *now*, and He's in you. He's in me. And His presence fills this place and fills your place and every place at the same time! Praise God! Hallelujah!

It's important that you have fellowship with believers. You know that, don't you? You're not an island unto yourself as a Christian. You're a member of the body. You're a member of the body of Christ. Christ in us and among us. Paul said the riches of the mystery is Christ in you and Christ among you. So He's in us and among us.

Let's read on a little bit. Verse 28, "*Whom we preach, warning every man, and teaching every man in all wisdom; that we may present every man perfect in Christ Jesus.*" Boy, that's quite a Scripture, isn't it? For most people, that's a big leap to believe that, but it says **we are *perfect* in Christ Jesus. Perfection is found in Him.** Remember, you and I are perfect *in Him.*

That word "perfect" there doesn't mean without human flaw. It means completeness in Christ. We're perfect in Him, having all that it takes to grow into full maturity and the full measure of the stature of Christ—perfect.

It reminds me of when a little baby is born and there's no problem. That little baby is perfect. He's got all his little fingers and toes and fingernails. That baby's perfect—he's got a heart, eyes, brains—that baby is perfect. If there's no problem from the birth standpoint, that baby is perfect and has everything that little one needs to become a full-grown man or woman. Everything is there. And that's the meaning of this verse—that you have everything you need to fulfill God's plan and purpose for your life. Glory to God. Hallelujah!

There are no birth defects in the new birth. Now, you as a Christian may have some challenges and some issues in your life. Listen, we're still adjusting to the new creation realities and dealing with some issues sometimes. People come from different backgrounds and different problems, but *in Christ* is a solution for all people, for all things, for all time. Praise God! Hallelujah! Thank you, Jesus! Amen!

As you and I begin to acknowledge the perfection that's in Christ, that perfection begins to work on any imperfection, moving it out of the way, and Christ rises up and lives big within our hearts. And then speak it out. Hallelujah!

It's so important that we understand that we have what it takes to be all God's called us to be. And as we acknowledge the good things in Christ, it becomes more and more effectual. Are you getting this? It becomes more and more effectual when you rise up and say, "I am a new creature in Christ Jesus. Old things have passed away. All things become new." You're acknowledging what God has done, and it overrides what the world has done and what the enemy has tried to do. In Christ we are free to be everything He's called us to be. So in that sense, we are perfect in Christ. Praise God! Hallelujah! Thank you, Jesus! Amen!

THE ENERGY OF GOD

I love this next verse, verse 29, I just want you to see this. This is Paul, the guy that wrote two-thirds of the New Testament, and he writes, "*Whereunto* [for this cause] *I also labour, striving according to his working, which worketh in me mightily*" (Colossians 1:29, brackets TM). He said, "This is the reason that I live. This is why I'm called. This is what I do. I strive with God's energy." That word is "energeia," the energy of God. He's saying, "I strive with God's energy, and it's working in me mightily, so I can let everybody know God did something in Christ for you, and that changes everything. Step into God's perfection in Christ."

He said, "This is my main message. It is what I teach and what I preach wherever I go." *Perfection* doesn't mean that there's not a human flaw, but it means there is a completeness in Christ that is ours today that helps us become full-grown, mature, strong, and aware of who we are in Him.

That's why Brother Hagin said, "One of the fastest ways, if not the fastest way to grow as a Christian is to find out who you are in Christ and begin to write down *in Him, in whom, and in Christ* Scriptures and confess that's who I am. That's what I have." It'll cause you to grow spiritually more than anything else—that and walking in love. Those two things will guarantee spiritual growth.

Remember, God sees us in Christ. He does not measure us by our own self or by our own ability. He measures us by the grace, ability, mercy, and love of Jesus. He sees us in Christ. He sees us sinless. He sees us set free because He laid our sicknesses, our sins, and our poverty on Jesus. And we are perfect in Him. We've got everything in us now. It's pulsating. It's powerful.

If that baby keeps on eating, keeps on drinking, and keeps on being loved, that baby's going to grow. I'm surprised how fast they grow! I've got grandchildren already graduated from high school. Where did that come from? It wasn't that long ago they were just toddlers. But they had all they needed to be in the natural. And you've got what's in you to be all you need to be in God. You're perfect.

As a matter of fact, there's a Scripture that says we are fitted for glory. What does that mean? That means we've been made in Christ with the exact measurements it takes to wear the glory of the Lord. I am perfect in Christ. Would you mind saying that today, right where you are? "I am perfect in Christ."

A lot of people won't say it. Do you know why? They look in the mirror of the Word, and they see the wrong image. They may see Jesus, but they don't see themselves in Jesus in the image. They see their flaws and their shortcomings. They know what they've done, what they've said. They've made mistakes.

We've all made mistakes, but Jesus never made any. We didn't get into this deal based on our goodness but on His goodness and on His grace. So don't look at the old man in the mirror. When I say "the mirror," I mean the mirror of the Word. Don't look at the old you. Look at the new you in Christ in the mirror. And then begin to say, "How are you doing this morning? You're looking good, because you're in Christ!" And say, "That's who I am, and that's what I have." Instead of looking at yourselves, look at Jesus. See what He says, and see what He's done. Hallelujah!

JESUS LIFTED UP

I'm not saying that sometimes we don't have weaknesses that we're aware of, but remember, when we look at Jesus, He takes care of those things that need to be adjusted if our heart is really hungry and moving toward Him. I like to say it this way: "You can focus on the problem, or you can focus on your faith. You can look at the snake and the snakebite, or you can look at Jesus."

John 3:16 is probably the most familiar verse in the world, I suppose. But look at verse 14, "*And as Moses lifted up the serpent in the wilderness, even so must the Son of man be lifted up.*"

It's talking about Jesus being lifted up on the cross. As Moses lifted up the serpent in the wilderness, Jesus will be lifted up on the cross. Why? "*That whosoever believeth in Him...*" (John 3:15). There's an *in Him* in John's writing. As a matter of fact, John's writings have a lot of the *in Him* phrases in them, particularly in the little "Johns" back there in the back of your Bible.

"*That whosoever believeth in him should not perish, but have eternal life*" (John 3:15). Well, what does it mean as Moses lifted up the serpent in the wilderness? Numbers 21 is an Old Testament parallel that we need to understand. Numbers 21:7 says, "*Therefore the people came to Moses, and said, 'We have sinned.'*"

Well, what happened was they had begun to murmur and complain against God and against Moses. And they were saying things like, "You just brought us out here so we could die in the wilderness. I wish we'd have stayed in Egypt. At least we could have had some bread!" They were just complaining. "We don't even like this manna!"

The Bible said in verse six that God sent fiery serpents among the people that bit the people, and many of the people died. Therefore, they came to Moses, and they said, "*We have sinned for we have spoken against the Lord and against you. Pray unto the Lord that He take these serpents from us.*" And Moses prayed for the people.

Verse eight, "*And the Lord said unto Moses, Make thee a fiery serpent, and set it upon a pole: and it shall come to pass, that every one that is bitten, when he looks upon the serpent on the pole, he shall live*" (paraphrased). The Amplified says you have to look with an attentive, expectant, absorbing gaze.

So John said that was a type and shadow of Jesus being raised upon the cross, because we were all snake-bit by sin. Remember 1 Corinthians 15:22—in Adam all die; in Christ all are made alive. The only way to get out of Adam is to get into Christ. The way you get into Christ is by faith in the blood of Jesus. Hallelujah! Praise God.

You can't get rid of the snakebite any other way. That old bite of sin will stay there. The devil will torment you. He'll even try to gain ground on you. But I'm telling you if we'll lift up our eyes and look to the cross of Calvary, look to Jesus dying on that Cross for us, we experience new creation realities. (Remember that preposition "for" means substitution.) We look to Him dying for us and know that we died with Him—that our sin nature was destroyed. We're buried with Him. We're raised with Him to a new life. And now we're seated with Him in heavenly places. Amen! Glory to God! That is a new creation reality.

And that is what John was teaching right there in John chapter three. He said that what happened in Numbers was a type and shadow of Jesus coming and hanging on the cross for our sin. He became our sin. He took that sin. He took that old bite of sin upon himself, took our sickness, took our shame, took our poverty, and took our disease.

And he said, "If you'll look at Him and focus on Him [remember the Amplified says, "With attentive, expectant, absorbing gaze"] you'll be saved." Let me tell you something, the Cross deserves your full attention, because what happened there changed everything. He was wounded for our transgressions. He was bruised for our iniquity. The chastisement of our peace was upon Him, and with His stripes we are healed (Isaiah 53:5). Praise God! Hallelujah! Glory to God. This message changes everything!

I like what John said—when you believe in Him, that's when it takes place. It's the *in Him* factor, the *in whom* factor, the *in Christ* factor that changes everything. These little prepositions are so powerful when it comes to new creation realities. Thank God for Jesus! I love you, Jesus! Nobody else can do what He did. I don't mind just looking at Him every day, but He's not on that cross anymore. He's seated at the right hand of God.

And by, the way, you're seated there with Him.

PERFECTION IS FOUND IN CHRIST

So earlier Paul said, "This is what I do. I spend my time preaching this message so that people can understand their perfection is found in Jesus." People have tried to be perfect in themselves—perfect weight, perfect height, perfect measurement, perfect this, perfect that. And that's fine, but you know that perfection is really found only in Christ. So Paul said, "That's what I do. That's how I spend my life. That's where my focus is—trying to present every man, woman, boy, and girl with this knowledge of being perfect in Christ."

So let's go to Ephesians 1:2, which says this: "*Grace be to you, and peace, from God our Father, and from the Lord Jesus Christ.*" Grace and peace are found in Christ. Look at verse three, "*Blessed be the God and Father of our Lord Jesus Christ, who hath blessed us with all spiritual blessings in heavenly places in Christ.*" That's an *in Christ* Scripture.

It reminds me of my song:

I am blessed in the city.
I'm blessed in the field.
I'm blessed by His power.
I'm blessed to do His will. I'm blessed coming in.
I'm blessed going out.
I'm blessed to be a blessing.
Somebody ought to shout! Hey, I'm blessed!

Somebody saw this verse and said, "Well, that just means 'spiritual blessings.' When we get to heaven we'll be blessed." No, that's not what that verse means because it says, "*in Christ...in heavenly places.*" That doesn't mean we've got to wait till heaven to enjoy the blessing. As a matter of fact, when you study that word *spiritual*, there's a better translation: it's *supernatural* blessings. Supernatural means something that overrides the natural. **Who you are in Christ has overridden who you were in just your natural life.** It's made you a new creature, a new being, that never existed before. You've got the very nature of God in you—the genes of righteousness. Hallelujah!

And so because you are a new creature in Christ, then you're blessed in Christ with every supernatural blessing that supersedes the natural situation. Aren't you glad for that? There's no situation the world can throw at you that you and Jesus can't overcome. Hallelujah! I've got victory in Jesus. I've got supernatural help. I've got friends in high places.

So when you encounter the trials of life—and they come to everybody—don't fold up like a withered flower. Rise up in who you are in Christ and begin to declare the blessings of the Lord. These blessings are based on God's love in Christ for us. They supersede the natural circumstance.

Healing is a supernatural blessing. Prosperity is a supernatural blessing. Wisdom is a supernatural blessing. The Bible said in Christ He's made unto us wisdom. Think of all the things in life that we don't probably have the power to handle on our own, but God, by His Spirit and what He did in Christ, by the blood of the Lamb, works in us, for us, and through us and brings us through with flying colors and victory.

I didn't say it's always easy, but it is always victorious.

And I like this translation. It is my favorite translation of Ephesians 1:3. It says this, *"Blessed be the God and Father of our Lord Jesus Christ, who has blessed us in Christ with every spiritual blessing that heaven itself enjoys"* (Ephesians 1:3, Norlie). I'm blessed with every blessing that heaven itself enjoys.

What's in heaven, I get in my life because of Jesus. Actually, Jesus came to bring a little bit of heaven down here. We can really have days of heaven on the earth in our life in Christ. Praise God! If you don't believe that, you don't believe the Bible.

Jesus did something here and now so we could live above the storms of life. That doesn't mean you don't have trouble. Listen, John 16:33, I'll quote it to you. Jesus said, "*In Me, you have peace....*" That's an *in Christ* Scripture. Where is our peace? In Christ. Just say it, "I have peace in Christ." That's who I am. That's what I have.

Storms of life come to everybody. It may not be a natural hurricane, but in a storm you're going through the wind and the waves and the challenges and what looks like a deficit. But remember, you are in Christ. So in the midst of that storm say, "I have peace in Christ." And then you tell the devil, "Shut up! And get out of my face in Jesus' name! Get under my feet!" You've got to take your authority. (By the way, your authority is a new creation reality). Your dominion has been restored in the name of the Lord. And if you don't tell the devil to shut up and back off, then he isn't going anywhere. Even though he's defeated, he still roams around as a lion, seeking whom he may devour. So, you've got to take your dominion. You've got to take your authority. Don't put up with the devil—*he's a toothless lion!*

Jesus said in John 16:33, "*In Me you have peace.*" Then He said, "*In the world, you'll have tribulation.*" In the world, you'll have tribulation.

I had a lady come to me one time and say, "Pastor, I want you to pray for me that I'll have no more trials."

I said, "Well, we'll need to pray that you die then."

She said, "No, no, no, I don't want that!"

I said, "Well, as long as you're on the earth, you're going to have some trials. But the good news is you've got victory because you're in Christ. Hallelujah!"

Oh, the wind may blow, and the rain may come, but if you're founded on the rock in Christ, you will stand. So stand tall through it all in Christ.

Jesus finished John 16:33 saying, "*Be of good cheer; I have overcome the world for you.*" You've got victory before the battles start! If you keep the devil in the arena of faith, you'll always win. If he gets you over in the arena of *feelings*, he'll whip up on you. Stand fast.

Jesus said, "*Be of good cheer.*" I like a good cheer, don't you? I like to be encouraged. Sometimes you've got to encourage yourself in the Lord. When I was in high school, we played a lot of sports. You know, we had cheerleaders. My favorite cheer was, "Hit 'em in the backbone. Sock 'em in the jaw. Put 'em in the cemetery! Rah, rah, rah!" Sometimes you just have to cheer yourself up. Hallelujah! "Jesus is Lord, ha, ha, ha! Jesus is Lord today." That's a good cheer. Devil, get out of my way! Ha! Jesus is Lord! Ha, ha, ha! Jesus is Lord today! Jesus is Lord! Ha, ha, ha! Devil get out of my way! Hallelujah!

He said we could have days of heaven on the earth. Yeah, you're going to have some trouble, but be of good cheer. He's already overcome it for you. Remember in the Old Testament, in Deuteronomy 11:18-25 (you might want to look that up) God told His people, "If you will hear My Word, if you will mark My Word, if you will put My Word in your mouth, in your mind, in your heart, in your life, if you'll teach it to your children, talk about it when you come in, when you go out. Talk about it when you sit down. Talk about it when you lie down" (TM highly paraphrased version). He said, "You just keep My Word, your children and you will have days of heaven on the earth" (Deuteronomy 11:18-25, paraphrased). Praise God.

God said the Old Covenant believers could have days of heaven on the earth through hearing and receiving His Word. But we have a better covenant than they did!

Jesus *is* the Word. We have received Jesus into our heart. That is the mystery that Paul was preaching—*Christ in you; you in Christ.* And because we receive that Word and now we acknowledge that, and now we understand that, and now we are putting that forth, I tell you days of heaven are ours to enjoy on planet earth. Hallelujah! Praise God!

Is heaven real? Yeah. Are we going there someday? Yeah. But I tell you, we don't have to have hell down here before we get to heaven. We can have days of heaven here. We can have dominion over the devil, over disease, over poverty, over all that stuff—*here.* Praise God. Hallelujah!

In Christ is where that life is at. So as you look at *in Christ* Scriptures, you'll find out that God has something better for you and me than He had for His people back then. Not because He didn't love them, but because they didn't have the blood of Jesus. **We have a better covenant based on better promises, bought by better blood.** It's not the blood of bulls and goats. He is the Lamb of God. Hallelujah! Thank you, Jesus! Praise God!

First Peter 1:18-19 said we're not redeemed with silver and gold, but we are redeemed with the precious blood of Jesus. So let me just challenge us with this: Why don't we just begin to enjoy our redemption? Don't worry so much. Cast all your care over on the Lord for He cares for you. Take authority over that devil. Tell him to get out of your face. Turn your eyes on Jesus. Begin to acknowledge every good thing that's in you in Christ and watch what happens. Praise the Lord! Hallelujah! Glory to God.

GOD CHOSE YOU

Let's pick back up with Ephesians 1:4, which says, "*According as he hath chosen us in him before the foundation of the world, that we should be holy and without blame before him in love.*" So verse three said we're blessed with every blessing heaven enjoys. And then Paul said, "We didn't choose Him. He chose us. He chose us *in Him* before the foundation of the world."

You know, you're not here by accident. You're here, right where you are, by divine destiny. You're called and chosen by God "*before the foundation of the world, that we should be holy and without blame before him in love*" (Ephesians 1:4). That sounds perfect to me. Doesn't that sound perfect? Without blame? If you had a test score without blame, that means you're *perfect.* Jesus took the test for you!

Well, Paul writes that God chose us in Him without blame. He chose us in Him to be holy. I'm holy in Him. Now, a lot of people won't say that. They think holiness is based on what you do. Now, there is right living; I understand that part. But listen, this thing is not brought to pass just by what I *do*. It's brought to pass by what *He has done.* And I get myself conformed to His image through acknowledging every good thing that is in me in Christ Jesus. Hallelujah!

I've got one song that says,

"Conformed to His image,
I look like the Son.
I've been made His righteousness
by faith in the Holy One.
I don't act like the devil.
He is not my boss.
I've been redeemed, restored, reborn by the power of the cross."

God said I stand before Him in Christ perfect, holy, and without blame. Thank you, Jesus! Glory to God!

I don't know about you, but that sort of makes me feel as bold as a lion—that I can stand in the presence of God because He wants me there. He's invited me there. He's made a way for me to get there and be there. He's not mad that I show up. That's what Jesus came for—to open up heaven to all who would dare to believe. So it makes me bold as a lion.

Proverbs 28:1 says, "*The wicked man flees when no one pursues, but the righteous are as bold as a lion*" (paraphrased). Are you the righteousness of God in Christ? Then you can be bold. Boldness is not arrogance. Boldness is confidence in the grace, love, mercy, and provision of God. I belong to the household of God, and so do you! Hallelujah!

I'm bold as a lion. I'm casting my cares on the Lord. I can stand in His presence. I'm not filled with fear. Second Timothy 1:7, "*God has not given us a spirit of fear, but power, love, and a sound mind.*" I'm not timid. I'm not fearful. I'm not depressed. Does any of that stuff ever try to come at me? Well, sure. It'll try to come at you, too. But rise up in Christ and declare, "I am in Christ, set free. In Christ I have the victory! I'm welcomed into the family of God. I am holy and without blame. I'm perfect in Christ." Hallelujah! Glory to God. Amen.

Look at Romans chapter eight, which we will visit again later in the book. All of these Scriptures are so powerful that we want to go back to them time and again to uncover more. Romans 8:1 says, "*There is therefore now no condemnation to them which are in Christ.*" Are you in Christ? If you're born again, you're in Christ. So therefore, there's now no condemnation in you. So rise up! Let go of that sense of failure, or guilt, or shame. Learn to forgive yourself. God has forgiven you.

Hebrews chapter 10 says that He remembers our sin no more. So why do you and I remember it and let it torment us when we make a mistake or go back and think on something we did even before we got saved? That thing's long gone. You're free from that. I know there are some consequences that happen because of mistakes we make, but don't carry the guilt and the shame and the fear around with you. Let go of that.

Use this Scripture as a good thing God did in you—that according to the law of the Spirit of life in Christ, I have no condemnation. I have a chapter entitled, "Zero Condemnation," but right now I want you to see this in the light of being bold as a lion to enter Daddy God's throne room. Praise God. Hallelujah!

ACCEPTED IN THE BELOVED

We'll close out this chapter back in Ephesians 1 again. I want us to get this part. We were at verse four. Paul said, "*According as he hath chosen us in him before the foundation of the world, that we should be holy and without blame before him in love.*"

He goes on, "*Having predestined us unto the adoption of children by Jesus Christ to himself, according to the good pleasure of his will*" (verse 5).

In other words, God did it because He wants to. You are wanted! You are loved! You are invited! You are crowned with glory and honor! It's God's good pleasure to give you the kingdom. It's God's good pleasure to work in you. Hallelujah! Praise God.

But you have to let these things *be*, let them grow, and acknowledge them.

And then verse six says this: "*To the praise of the glory of his grace wherein he hath made us accepted in the beloved.*" That's one of my favorite Scriptures. I'm accepted in the beloved. I am also the beloved. I like to say I'm the beloved because I "be loved." You "be loved"! Hallelujah!

So realize simply that, in Christ, you belong. In Christ, you are accepted. I don't know who's rejected you. I don't know what you've gone through, but I can tell you this—God has not rejected you. And you are fully founded in His grace in Him and everything that Jesus did at Calvary, which belongs to you. You are a member of His family. That's who you are. That's what you have.

CHAPTER 5:

ABSOLUTE LIFE

I want to go back to the book of Ephesians. We left off here in the last chapter, and I want to explore a little bit more about this first chapter of Ephesians because it is so rich.

This chapter is so powerful. It talks about *in Christ* realities and how you and I belong to the family of God. From the previous chapter, you know I belong here—in the presence of God, in the family of God in Christ. I'm wanted here. God wants me. I live in the kingdom. I belong. I'm wanted. When you are in Christ, you are wanted, part of a family, and a member of the kingdom!

Never think that God doesn't want you and doesn't have a plan for your life! **You are accepted in the beloved, and He chose you before the foundation of the world!**

Every life varies a little bit—how we were raised and what we went through. Let me tell you something, the blood of Jesus covers it all. Hallelujah! Receive these new creation realities into your life and begin to acknowledge them. That's who I am. That's what I have. No matter your past, *in Christ* is who you are now.

So let's go back to Ephesians chapter one again and pick up where we left off with verse five, "*Having predestinated us unto the adoption of children by Jesus Christ to himself, according to the good pleasure of his will.*"

In other words, God made a plan to bring us into the family through Jesus Christ. We are born of God. It uses the word "adoption" there because we have a legal document of adoption called the New Testament, and it is signed by the blood of Jesus. But we're actually *reborn of God.* You know, when you're adopted in the world's system, you're brought into that family but you weren't fathered normally by the father of that family. But we're fathered by God! So He just made a way in Christ for us to be received into the family.

I love that word "adoption" because you don't adopt a child unless you want one. So that right there proves that we're wanted in God's mind. Plus, He said He did it according to the good pleasure of His will. Listen, God didn't *have* to do anything! God is God. But because He is love, He was compelled by that love to reach out to the lost and dying who we were without God in the world, and He brought us into His family by the new birth and then gave us a legal adoption that can never be annulled.

Then He said that's "*to the praise of the glory of his grace*" (Ephesians 1:6). Praise God! We've got something to really get happy about. We praise God for His glorious grace. His grace reached us. His grace touched us. His grace provided for us. And whoever you are, wherever you may be, God's grace is enough to pick you up and bring you in. Praise the Lord! Hallelujah!

"*To the praise of the glory of his grace, wherein he hath made us accepted in the beloved*" (Ephesians 1:6). By His grace, He made us accepted. There are a lot of definitions for "grace," but here's one of my favorite definitions: "grace is God's divine want-to."

He did it because He wanted to! He provided our redemption in Christ. Think about the magnitude of that statement. Provided our redemption in Christ—"*in whom,*" Paul says. Verse seven says "*In whom we have redemption through his blood....*" That's a new creation reality. "*In whom we* [say "I" as you read it] *have redemption through his blood, the forgiveness of sins, according to the riches of his grace*" (Ephesians 1:7, brackets TM).

God's grace is sufficient. God's forgiveness is for your past and your future. There is provision for you for every sin for all time. And you can walk in the reality of that forgiveness. You can accept that forgiveness. When you make a mistake as a believer, you can say, "God, I missed it" and receive that forgiveness because you've already been forgiven. Don't let the devil hold you down. Don't let Him rope you down like a calf in the rodeo! Get up and be free from all the snares of the enemy because of the grace of God, the blood of Christ, and the redemption that we have in Jesus.

We are redeemed in Him. Hallelujah! Our sins are forgiven according to the riches of His grace. His grace reached back into your past, reaches into your future, and is forgiveness for you today. Receive that forgiveness. Forgive yourself.

Many people have a struggle forgiving themselves. There's things that I'm ashamed of, particularly before I was saved and some after I was saved, but I'm not going to live in the shadow of my sins or my mistakes. I'm going to live in the light of the cross. I've been by that empty tomb, and it's still empty. Hallelujah!

You say, "Well, I've never been to Jerusalem." But you can go by the tomb in the Bible. Go to Matthew, Mark, Luke, and John. They said it's still empty. If it's still empty, that means you're alive in Christ, you've got the victory, and you ought to rejoice about it. Praise God! Hallelujah! You're forgiven. You're set free by the blood of the Lamb according to His grace.

Verse 8, "*Wherein he hath abounded toward us in all wisdom and prudence.*" Because of His grace and in His grace, God was able to run *to* us. He didn't wait for us to run to Him. He didn't wait for you to be perfect and flawless before He saved you. As a matter of fact, the Bible says, "*While we were yet sinners, Christ died for us*" (Romans 5:8). Hallelujah! That means grace allowed God to run *to you.* He's a holy God. He's a righteous God. There's no flaw in perfect God, but His grace allowed Him to run to you in love, accept you, forgive you, and make all things new.

The Amplified Bible says, "*He lavished his grace on us with all wisdom and prudence*" (Ephesians 1:8, paraphrased). Lavished—I like that word. We don't use that much, but to lavish means to give without limits. Lavish is marked by extravagance.

Did you know everything about your redemption is *extravagant*? It's pretty extravagant for God to become a man. To walk this earth and be sinless and go to the cross as our substitute, that's pretty extravagant. To go to hell, to suffer for us, to be raised from the pit by the power of God, taking our sin, taking our punishment, and our penalty, and coming alive through the power of God's righteousness and love for us—that's all pretty extravagant.

Is there anything too hard for God to do for you? I don't think so. The Bible said, "All things are possible to him who believes" (Mark 9:23 NKJV). Because we are in Christ, God has emptied His wrath upon His Son, and He has showered His blessing—or lavished His blessing—upon us.

In Hebrews chapter one it says that Jesus Christ is the heir and rightful owner of all things, and you are in Him. We are in Him, the heirs and rightful owners of all things. That means you've got somebody on your side. The Bible says we are kings and priests unto God. We are somebody in Him. He has made us full of His life. He has filled us with His Spirit. He is helping us today to overcome and understand who we are in Him. Praise God. Hallelujah! We're made full in Him, perfect in Him. We've come to fullness of life. In Christ we are filled with the Godhead—the Father, Son, and the Holy Ghost. Hallelujah! And we reach full spiritual stature because we're perfect in Christ with everything we need to grow into the full image of the glory of God.

THE MYSTERY OF HIS WILL

Look at verse nine. Paul says this: "*Having made known unto us the mystery of his will, according to his good pleasure which he hath purposed in himself.*" Verse 10-11 goes on, "*That in the dispensation of the fulness of times he might gather together in one all things in Christ, both which are in heaven, and which are on earth; even in him* [even *in Him*]: *In whom* [There's an *in whom.*] *also we have obtained an inheritance, being predestined according to the purpose of him...*" (brackets TM). We are predestined in Him according to the purpose of Him (verse 11). You and I find our fulfillment and our purpose—our destiny—in Christ. And as we acknowledge who He is and what He has done and thank Him for that and worship Him for that, He begins to work out all things according to the counsel of His will, "*That we should be to the praise of his glory, who first trusted in Christ*" (verse 12).

Colossians 2:9-10 says, "*For in Him the whole fullness of Deity (the Godhead) continues to dwell in bodily form [giving complete expression of the divine nature]. And you are in Him, made full and having come to fullness of life [in Christ you too are filled with the Godhead—Father, Son and Holy Spirit—and reach full spiritual stature]. And He is the Head of all rule and authority [of every angelic principality and power]*" (AMPC).

That's a definition of perfect. We're perfect in Christ. We've got all that we need from Him to be all that He's called us to be. So acknowledge who you are in Christ.

There's a little song that I sing sometimes. I had this song for many years, but it just goes like this:

"I am in Him.

The Lord Jesus Christ made full and have come to fullness of life.

I am a new creature created in Christ by my Father God.

And I too am filled with the Godhead—Father, Son, and Holy Ghost.

I too am filled with the Godhead—Father, Son, and Holy Ghost.

I am in Him, the Lord Jesus Christ, made full and have come to fullness of life.

I am a new creature created in Christ by my Father God."

Hallelujah!

LIFE AND LIGHT IS IN HIM

Now let's go over to the Gospel of John and talk about life in Christ. John chapter one is one of my favorite chapters in the Bible. It's powerful. Let's start from verse one: "*In the beginning was the Word, and the Word was with God, and the Word was God. The same was in the beginning with God. All things were made by him; and without him was not any thing made that was made. In him was life*" (John 1:1-4) There's a good *in Him* Scripture. "*In Him was life; and the life* [that was in Him] *was the light of men*" (verse 8, brackets TM).

In Him was life and in Him is life. The life of God is in Him. And that life that is in Him becomes the light of man.

So there's life in Him. There's light in Him. There's love in Him. There's joy in Him. There's help in Him. There's peace in Him. We've touched on all these things. It's *in Christ.* I have peace *in Him.* I have life *in Him.* Praise God! In Him dwells the fullness of God, so in me dwells the fullness of God. I'm in Him; He's in me. I like to say, "I in Him. He in me. We in them. They in we. What a glorious place to be—hid with Christ in God." Hallelujah!

The life of God is in us in Christ. And that life of God, or the life of love—God is love—is in us to love Him with and to love others. As a matter of fact, that's how we walk in the light—by walking in love. And that's the way the life of God is manifest in us: by walking in love. We understand that the life of God comes from God Himself and that we have that life because of what Jesus has done.

First John 4:19 says that, "*We love Him because He first loved us.*" It goes back to just what we're saying—God didn't wait for us to get everything in order before He ran to us. He ran to us with His grace. He ran to us in His love. He wrapped His arms around us, and He made us new creatures in Christ Jesus.

"*We love Him because He first loved us*" (1 John 4:19). Verse 20 says, "*If a man say, I love God, and hateth his brother, he is a liar.*" It says you can't love the one whom you haven't seen if you don't love the one whom you have seen. This is an important issue when it comes to walking in new creation realities. The love of God is shed abroad in our heart. And there is a love limit on your life, by the way.

You can only go as far in God as you are committed to walk in the commandment of love. I like to say it this way: "revelation can only flourish in an atmosphere of love." So we're loving God, but we're also loving one another. We're loving God; we're also loving ourselves.

We're letting the life that's in Him flow through us. In Him was life, and that life is giving me light. I am not walking in the darkness. There is no reason to stumble walking in the darkness when you walk in the life that's in Christ, because that life will produce light, and that light will keep us from walking in the darkness. And if we love one another, then we walk in the light because in the light is where God has called us to stay.

So acknowledging the life of God, accepting the light of Christ, and walking in the love of God is part of new creation realities. I love Him because He first loved me. I love you because God loved me. I can walk in the light of that love, and that light that's produced in me because of Christ is so powerful. It swallows up death in all of its forms. Hallelujah!

There's nothing the enemy can attempt to do that you and I cannot overcome in Christ because life in Christ is greater than all the death in the devil and every attempt that he tries to hinder or to stop the plan of God. We are victorious in this life. The Bible talks about that. The light of God comes because of this life. Liberty in Christ comes because of this life. Freedom comes because of this life that's in Christ that now has come into me. I'm alive with the life of God. You have freedom to see, freedom to do, and freedom to be the new you. Hallelujah! Happy new you in Christ Jesus.

THE ETERNAL GOOD LIFE

John 1:4 said, "*In him was life.*" That's an *in Him* Scripture. In Him was life, that life is in me because I'm in Him. And that life swallows up death in all of its form, swallows up disease in all of its form, and swallows up fear in all of its form—the life of God is powerful. As a matter of fact, that Greek word for life is the Greek word *zoe*. In Him was *zoe*. In Him is *zoe*. And there's *zoe* in me today. Praise God, I've got *zoe* life in me.

As we meditate on who we are in Him, *zoe* is released because there's life in Him. Hallelujah! The word "meditate" means "to study, to ponder, to speak." So when we say "meditate on the Word," we study it. We think about it. We speak it out. And the *speaking* part is vital. Because the door of faith swings on two hinges—believing and speaking—so the speaking part is vital. As we meditate on who we are in Him and as we acknowledge—which is the speaking part—who we are in Him, then *zoe* life is released.

The definition of *zoe* life in the simple form is "the God-kind of life." It's unending life. It's unparalleled life. It has no equal. It's not just life in quantity, but life in *quality*, meaning that it's not just eternal life; it's eternal *good* life. Who wants eternal bad life? Hallelujah!

Listen, if you leave this world not knowing Christ, you're still going to be an eternal creature, but it's not going to be good. Hell is not a happy place. It's not created for you. Jesus came to set you free from the clutches and the hands of the enemy. So if you don't know Jesus as Lord, please receive your forgiveness. Simply cry out, "Jesus, have mercy on me." Receive His love, and receive the God kind of life—eternal good life, eternal blessed life, eternal *Jesus* life! Hallelujah! Praise God!

In John 10:10 Jesus said, "*The thief cometh not, but for to steal, and to kill, and to destroy.*" You can always tell when something is from the devil or not. If it's trying to steal, kill, destroy, hold back, push down, or condemn—that's not from the Lord. The Lord's not pushing you down, pushing you back, holding you back, stealing your children, or stealing your health. That's the enemy trying to get his way. Tell him to shut up and back off!

Jesus said this: "*I am come that they* [us] *might have life* [that's *zoe*], *and that they might have it more abundantly*" (verse 10, brackets TM). *More* abundantly is more than abundant—*more* abundantly. What does that mean? **Life without limits is available in Christ!**

Can you imagine absolute life, meaning the absence of anything that is in any way detrimental or death or destroying or discouraging? Heaven is a place of *absolute life*. There are no tears, fears, sickness, or disappointments in heaven. You're in the presence of absolute life.

God is love. God is life. God is in me, and He's *in you*. He's not just there, waiting; He's *in you!*

I used to sing that little song all the time:

God is love.
God is light.
God is in me.
I'm not walking in the night 'cause God is in me.
I've been changed, rearranged,
Oh, He is in me.
Oh, praise His name
He's still the same, and He's in me.

I just kept emphasizing He's in me. He's in me. He's in you today too. And we are in Him.

So as we meditate on this *zoe* life, it is life more abundantly. That means there's *more than you can handle!* You can't contain it all. It just bubbles out and bubbles over, bubbles into your family, bubbles into your finances, bubbles into your situations, bubbles into your body—just bubbles in everywhere. We can get so full of life it can change an entire city! Praise the Lord! Glory to God! Hallelujah!

It's more than you need. It's life without limits, more than enough. This is the kind of life that God has given us in Christ Jesus. In Him was life and that life is in me. That's who I am. That's what I have.

THE LIFE IS IN THE SON

Let's go now to 1 John 5:11. He said, "*And this is the record, that God hath given to us eternal life* [*zoe*]." Remember, the word *zoe*, means quality and quantity. It's also eternally good life, or you could say eternally *God* life. So let's read that again, "*And this is the record, that God hath given to us eternal* [and good] *life* [*zoe*] *and this life is in his Son*" (verse 11 brackets TM). That's a new creation reality right there.

I'm a new creation filled with the life of God. I don't just have temporary life. I've got something greater than temporary life. I've got eternal *zoe*. In fact, I'm never going to die. No, I've been crucified with Christ. You can't kill a dead man. I'm raised to life. The fear of death has been broken over us in Christ. Jesus came to deliver those who were held in bondage by the fear of death (Hebrews 2:15). Hallelujah! Praise God!

Why do you think the Bible says, "*Precious in the sight of the Lord is the death of His saints*" (Psalm 116:15)? That's because it's not really a death. It's just a translation. It's just a vacating of this old body and moving to heaven. Praise the Lord! Hallelujah!

Temporary life for some people seems to be really great. But you know what? If they don't have Jesus, they don't really have anything. You know the Bible says, "*What does it profit a man if he gains the whole world but loses his soul?*" (Mark 8:36, paraphrased) That's sad. We don't have to do that. Nobody has to do that. Jesus died for all people, for all time, and cleansed every one of us. If you know Him today, there's something greater in you than temporary life. The blessings of the Lord are for here and now, but we've got life in us that will never go out. The eternal life of God has lit us up, and that light will never go out. And this life is in His Son.

Look at verse 12—John makes it real clear: "*He who has the Son has life; he who does not have the Son of God does not have life*" (1 John 5:12). You're either in Adam or in Christ. There is no in-between. In Adam all die. In Christ all are made alive (see 1 Corinthians 15:22). If you've got Jesus, you've got this *zoe* life, and you can put that life to work. You can acknowledge that good work that God's put in you. You can confess with your mouth "in Him was life and the life was the light of men." Realize that you've been lit up for eternity. Your light's never goin' out! Hallelujah! It's going to get brighter, and brighter, and brighter because you acknowledge every good thing that's in you in Christ.

Here's another song I used to sing about in Christ:

Living in Christ, alive, alive.

Living in God's love.

In heavenly places hid in God

I am far above.

Oh, I'm living in Christ,

So God's living in me.

His life, His nature, and ability.

Living in Christ, living God in me

Alive, alive, alive!

Do you know what happens when you sing that song or something like that every day? The life of God will begin to radiate from your being working in you and working for you, fixing stuff. You got any stuff you'd like to see fixed? The *zoe* of God can fix it. Hallelujah! Praise God.

I think we need a Jesus takeover, a Holy Ghost takeover. I believe we need a *zoe* takeover, a life takeover where the life of God just floods our life and fills our life like John G. Lake. Lake was overseas, and people started getting the bubonic plague. And he ministered to many of them, but he never got the disease. And when the doctors got there, they said, "How did you not happen to get this disease?" He said, "Well, the life of God in me protected me." They said, "What do you mean?" He said, "Well, I'll show you." And they took some of that germ-filled, disease-filled foam that comes out of the mouth of the people that die of the bubonic plague, and they put it on his hand. And he put his hand under a microscope and right in front of their eyes, the disease and germs *died*. He had such faith in the life of God! The *zoe* of God was in Him! He said when it touches this body that's filled with *zoe*, it will *die*! The *zoe* will cause it to go away. Hallelujah! *Alive, alive, alive, I'm living in Christ.*

YOU ARE HIS HANDIWORK

So this quality of life, this quantity of life, is ours in Christ. It's a good life. It's what God gave us. Ephesians 2:10 says this, "*For we are His workmanship, created in Christ Jesus for good works, which God prepared beforehand that we should walk in them.*"

We are His workmanship. We are His handiwork. You remember God, in the beginning, breathed life. In the New Testament we'd say He breathed *zoe* into us in the new birth. The life of God is in us. Hallelujah! We are His handiwork, His workmanship. The Amplified says "*handiwork*," and I love that because that implies that He is a hands-on God. He didn't delegate Calvary to an angel or to someone else. He actually sent Himself in His Son to take care of business—to produce this *zoe* life for us. Hallelujah! He took care of the devil, disease, debt, doubt, depression, and all difficulties. He gave us the victory in Christ Jesus. We are His handiwork, recreated in Christ unto good works, which God hath foreordained that we should walk in them living the good life.

You and I are not here by accident. It's by divine design. It's by divine destiny. We're not even living in this space in time by accident. We have been planted here by the purpose of God. He has a plan for my life. He has a plan for your life, and the Bible says that plan is hidden in God, in Christ. Remember, it's not hidden from us. It's hidden *for* us. And we can discover that plan. One of the *in Him* Scriptures, Colossians 2:3 says, "*In whom are hidden all the treasures of wisdom and knowledge.*" God has something in Christ for us today. We are His workmanship. He put this together. He placed you on this planet. You're perfect. You can be everything He's called you to be because of Christ. Hallelujah!

We can activate God's plan and purpose with our *voice*. We can affirm and acknowledge every good thing that's in us in Christ Jesus. As we do, those things that are hidden for us come to the forefront, and we begin to see Christ in us the hope of glory. Praise God. Hallelujah!

You know you're a resurrected man or woman. We're alive with the life of God forevermore. We have heaven life, God life, *zoe* life, eternal life, and good life, not just temporary life. But it affects our temporary life here. It makes our temporary life much better. We can walk in the reality of our redemption here and now healed, well, strong, rich, free, happy.

Colossians 3:1-3 says this, "*If ye then be risen with Christ, seek those things which are above, where Christ sitteth on the right hand of God. Set your affection on things above, not on things on the earth. For ye are dead, and your life is hid with Christ in God.*" Hallelujah!

I like to say, "Seek and speak those things that concern you in Christ where He's seated at the right hand of God." Seek those things that are in Christ. Set your affection on Him and the things that are in Him and who He is and what He's done. Hallelujah!

I know I'm in love with Jesus. I'm sure you are, too. He is the shepherd of my soul. And then you see yourself in Him, because you are in Him, and He's in you. That's what the new creation reality is about—what God did in Christ, and what Christ is doing in us. And when that happens, then the new creation realities become a reality in your life. That's pretty simple, right? It's the way I think, the way I talk, the way I walk, the way I live, the way I give, the way I do. It all happens because of who He is and what He's done. So I like to say, "Seek, set, and see, and the new creation realities become a reality."

For He said, "*Ye are dead, and your* [real, new] *life is hid with Christ in God*" (Colossians 3:3, brackets TM). I'm dead to the world. I'm alive unto God. I'm dead to the world, and my life is hidden with Christ in God my Father. Hallelujah! "I in Him, and He in me. We in them, and they in we." What a glorious place to be hidden with Christ in God. It's like this song I mentioned before:

Because I'm dead to the world and my life is hid
with Christ.
In God my Father, Hallelujah!
I in Him, and He in me.
We in them, and they in we.
What a glorious place to be
Hid with Christ in God.

This is the secret place of the Most High! It's something hidden in Christ that we are discovering, that we are uncovering, that we are disclosing. We are new creatures in Christ. We have a new creation reality that's become a reality. We are living in Him. He's living in us. And the same life that's in Him is in us. It's not only long eternal life, but it's good life. It's God life.

Ephesians 2:10 in the Amplified Bible says it this way: "*For we are God's [own] handiwork.*" I love that personal side of this Amplified translation. God personally got involved in our redemption by Himself coming in His Son. "*Recreated in Christ Jesus*" (Ephesians 2:10). I like that too. We're recreated in Christ Jesus, brand new. Recreated—not re-worked, not rebuilt, but recreated. Listen, the Amplified says, "*That we may do those good works which God predestined (planned beforehand) for us*" (verse 10). God's got some things for you to do. How are you going to do them? In Christ as we acknowledge Ephesians 2:10, these things become a reality. Hallelujah!

"*[Taking paths] which He prepared ahead of time], that we should walk in them [living the good life which He prearranged and made ready for us to live]* (in Christ)" (verse 10, parenthesis TM). God's working in me, God's working through me, and God's working for me. He is bringing His purposes to pass in my life. I acknowledge every good thing in me. I am His handiwork. I'm recreated in Christ. I'm doing those works He's planned for me to do. I'm taking paths He prepared ahead of time. I'm living the good life, which He prearranged and made ready for me to live. That's who I am, and that's what I have. Hallelujah! Praise God!

THE GOD OF BEFORE YOU GET THERE

Well, you say, "I haven't seen all that!" Well, you haven't seen it all yet, but it's coming to pass because God is causing your faith to be effectual as you acknowledge every good thing that's in you in Christ Jesus.

Did you know **God goes into your future and makes provision *before you get there*?** That is the literal translation of Jehovah Jireh, by the way. Jehovah Jireh, our provider, literally means "the One who goes into our future and makes provision before we get there." There is nothing that ever can come your way that God has not made provision for.

Before you were born, He knew you. He called you by your name. He's got a plan and prepared a way for you to walk in. Walk in that reality by faith. Begin to declare, "God knows who I am. God knows what I need, and He made provision for me already!" Hallelujah! God goes into my future and makes provision before I get there. So no matter what challenge comes upon me, or what trial I'm going through, God's been there before I got there, and He made provision for me. The devil cannot sneak up on me. The Lord has turned my captivity to freedom, and I have the victory. The devil can't stop me. God is for me. I win! That's who I am. That's what I have. Hallelujah!

One more verse and we'll close out this chapter. Proverbs 3:5-6 says, "*Trust in the Lord with all thine heart; and lean not unto thine own understanding. In all thy ways acknowledge him* [who He is and what He's done, and who you are in Christ], *and he shall direct thy paths*" (Proverbs 3:5-6, brackets TM).

Acknowledging God and who we are in Christ is the way we align ourselves with the new realities we have through Jesus. He has given us absolute life, and it is a path that is definitely worth walking! It's the life you were meant to live!

CHAPTER 6:

REJOICE IN THE LORD

We ended our last chapter talking about Proverbs 3:5-6. And that really goes together with one of our core Scriptures in Philemon 1:6 where it says the communication of our faith becomes effectual as we acknowledge every good thing that's in us in Christ Jesus. We're learning to acknowledge, or to speak, who we are in Christ.

Proverbs 3:5-6 says, "*Trust in the Lord with all thine heart*"—*in the Lord*. That's an *in Him* Scripture, isn't it?—"*and lean not to your own understanding. In all your ways acknowledge him, and he shall direct your paths*" (paraphrased).

So as we acknowledge Him, acknowledge who He is and what He's done for us, then those paths become apparent that we are to walk in, and we can live the good life, which we learned He prearranged and made ready for us to live in Christ.

If we ever had a reason to rejoice, it's because we're in Christ, because, remember, in Adam all die, in Christ all are made alive (1 Corinthians 15:22). So no matter what you're going through, your name is written in the Lamb's book of life, and that's the number one reason you're to rejoice. So rejoice in Christ Jesus.

We've got the best deal going in Christ. It doesn't need any upgrades. It's done by Christ for all people for all time. We are perfect in Him. We've got a complete redemption, an everlasting release, and God is on our side. That's worth rejoicing over!

Let's read Philippians 4:4. It says this, "*Rejoice in the Lord always: and again I say, Rejoice.*" Other translations say, "Rejoice in the Lord every day." And that's Scriptural. This is the day the Lord has made; we will rejoice and be glad (Psalm 118:24). That doesn't mean just the Monday or the Tuesday or whatever day of the week you read that Scripture, although you can apply it to that. It actually means "the day in which we live, the time in which we live." God only has three days—He's got yesterday, today, and forever. We're living in today, so we're living in the day that the Lord has made in Christ, and we're to rejoice. Hallelujah!

Here's another translation, "Rejoice in the Lord on every occasion, or in every circumstance." In every circumstance, rejoice in the Lord? Why? Because God is on our side. We're in Christ. We've got victory guaranteed. I like to say this, "I sing because Jesus Christ is King. I shout because the Lord has brought me out. I dance because the devil ain't got a chance. I thank God I'm in Christ, and I've learned to rejoice."

When was the last time you did some dancing because of what Jesus did? That's a good question. We used to dance for the devil. We might as well dance because we're in Jesus! Somebody said Smith Wigglesworth, an old-time apostle who raised I don't know how many people from the dead, when asked, "How do you start your day?" said, "This is what I do. The moment I get out of bed, I dance before the Lord—high speed dancing for ten or twelve minutes." That's a pretty good way to start your day, isn't it? You can start your day dancing. He said, "I start my day dancing, telling God how much I love Him, how glad I am that I'm saved, how I am glad for my redemption. And I just praise Him and dance all around my room." And then he said, "I sit down and read the Bible for an hour. Then I get up and shower, get my instructions from God. And I go do my day."

So, why don't you try that? Start your day dancing. "*Rejoice in the Lord always; and again I say, rejoice.*" There's no better place to be than in Christ. So I rejoice in the Lord always. My position in him never changes. I rejoice that I'm in Him. I rejoice that He's in me. That's what He said to do. Praise the Lord.

An Old Testament Scripture, Nehemiah 8:10, says, "*Go your way, eat the fat, and drink the sweet, and send portions unto them for whom nothing is prepared: for this day is holy unto our Lord: neither be ye sorry; for the joy of the Lord is your strength.*" Well, here's a better translation in my opinion. It says, "*Rejoicing in the Lord is your strength*" (NABRE).

In other words, I need to express my joy, and one way I do that is in my rejoicing. So what am I rejoicing about? I'm rejoicing because I'm *in Christ*! Get happy over that. It may not look good right now. Whatever you're going through, and whatever you're dealing with that day, there may be a lot of pressure, a lot of demands on you, but don't lose your joy! Praise God. You're in Jesus! You're on your way to heaven! Your name's in the Lamb's Book of Life. You can rejoice over your condition and your position. What condition is that? Well, the condition is "*I am the righteousness of God in Christ.*" That's my condition; "*I'm the righteousness of God in Christ.*" What's my position? "*I'm seated in heavenly places with Him.*" I've been raised with Him and made to sit with Him in heavenly places. I've got a new condition and a new position, so everything is going to be alright! Praise God! Hallelujah!

So I'm going to rejoice. I'm not going to worry. Don't let circumstances take you out or dictate your condition or position. **You dictate to circumstances; they do not dictate to you.** The Bible said, "*Rejoice in the Lord.*" Praise God. Get happy about being in Jesus! Get happy about being saved. We can be happy in Jesus because we are redeemed.

WORSHIP IN THE SPIRIT

Look at Philippians 3:3, which says "*We are the* [covenant people] *which worship God in the spirit, and rejoice in Christ Jesus, and have no confidence in the flesh* [for our righteousness]" (Philippians 3:3 paraphrased, brackets TM).

He said there are three things that we covenant people ought to be doing. He said, "We ought to be worshipping God in the spirit." Jesus said, "*They that worship God, must worship Him in the spirit and in truth*" (John 4:24, paraphrased). That simply means that no matter where I am, I can worship God because where I am is a worship house because *I'm* the worship house. God lives in me. We come together in the church, in the building, but *we* personally are the body of Christ. He lives in *us*. So every day is a worship day. Don't wait till Sunday to worship God, worship Him every day because He's in you. Your body is the temple or the tabernacle of the Holy Spirit.

Then he said, secondly, covenant people rejoice in Christ Jesus. This ought to be a mark of our Christianity—our joy. Jesus said, "*I have come that my joy might be in you, and that your joy might be made full*" (John 15:11, paraphrased).

So, one of the purposes that Jesus came was to give us "Jesus' joy." One of the marks of the believer is rejoicing. You say, "Well, I don't feel very happy today. I'm not feeling good. Things aren't looking too good." I understand that, but you can rejoice anyway because you're in Christ. You can rejoice because He has given you the victory. God always causes us to triumph in Him (2 Corinthians 2:14). Just start getting happy about that. Don't let the circumstance dictate your joy.

The Bible says, "*With joy shall we draw water from the wells of salvation*" (Isaiah 12:3, paraphrased). Joy becomes like a dipping bucket for us to draw up healing, draw up help, draw up peace, draw up all that we need from the well of salvation that Jesus has dug just for you and me. Remember, you are in Christ. You're not in Adam. That's a good reason to get glad.

And then third, he said, "You do not have to depend on your flesh for your righteousness." That is really good news because righteousness is a gift from God received by faith in Christ Jesus. It said in 2 Corinthians 5:21 that Him who knew no sin was made to be sin for us, that we might be made the righteousness of God in Him. I've got right standing with God. I am declared innocent. No more guilt. No more shame. No more defeat. Jesus is Lord. I'm the righteousness of God. He's extended Himself to me. His righteousness is in me. It's not just *on* me—though it is on me—but it's *in* me. I like to say that His gene of righteousness is in us. We're fathered by God. What's in Him has got in us.

Righteousness is a gift of God's great grace, and it comes to us at the new birth. We don't depend on our flesh, our works, our ability, or our goodness. Remember, our self-righteousness is as filthy rags. We depend on Jesus. He has become our righteousness. God has made Him to be sin for me, that I might be made His righteousness. He became a curse to restore my fellowship with

God. I've been delivered from Satan's power, and I partake this very hour of all that God has for me as a joint-heir with Christ.

Somebody says, "Well, I was just born that way," thinking to give an excuse for their behavior. No, no. You need to say, "I was *re*born *this* way. I was reborn the righteousness of God." Yes, you may bear the sinful past of our earthly lineage, but what about your Father in Heaven? His DNA has gotten into you! Start confessing that! Start talking God-talk over your life. Start seeking those things that are above. Speak out who you are. You are an heir of God and a joint heir with Jesus Christ. You are somebody in Christ going somewhere to do something *awesome* for God. And you can rejoice every day in the goodness of God.

JOINT HEIRS

Look over to Romans 8:16, which says this, "*The Spirit itself beareth witness with our spirit, that we are the children of God.*" That's called being born of God or born of the Spirit. When you accept Jesus Christ as Lord, you're born of God, born of the Spirit of God. Hallelujah! So, the Spirit bears witness that we are the children of God. "*And if children, then heirs; heirs of God, and joint-heirs with Christ*" (Romans 8:17).

Did you see that little "*with*" there? We just read over it most of the time, but that's an identification word. It magnifies a relationship. I have a relationship with Jesus, and He has shared His inheritance with me. He says I'm a *joint*-heir. I have access to His inheritance. Everything He has is mine. He said the Holy Spirit will reveal it to me if I'll let Him.

Jesus wants to share it all with you. That's why He came. That's what He did. That's who we are. That's what we have.

I'm an heir of God and a joint-heir with Christ, and I'm going to get happy about it! If somebody leaves you an inheritance, you're not sad about it, are you? You better not be. You ought to get happy and rejoice because we are joint-heirs with Jesus Christ! We rejoice in Christ that all things are provided for us in Him.

"With" means we're identified with Him in His death, His burial, His resurrection, His seating—I'm not done—*and* His Sonship. Praise the Lord! Hallelujah! Thank you, Jesus. Glory to God. Identify with His Sonship. I have become a son of God. You have become a son or a daughter of God in Christ. It would be good to acknowledge that and to rejoice about it! Say, "I am a child of God. I'm an heir of God. I'm a joint-heir with Christ. I've got equal access to the inheritance in Jesus' name." Hallelujah!

YOU ALREADY HAVE THE JOY, JUST ACT LIKE IT

I'm telling you, we're getting into something here that produces joy. And we've got something to rejoice about that we are *in Christ, with Christ,* and it's *through Christ* that we enjoy our inheritance.

Remember that no matter what trial you may be going through, victory is our *guarantee.* And you may go through persecution and pressure, but glory is on the way. Victory is in the way. There's coming a breakthrough day. So rejoice in the breakthrough day.

You may say, "Well, it isn't here yet."

Well, why don't you act like it's here? How would you act if you had what you were believing for? You'd get pretty happy. So why not start being happy now?

I know a story of a pastor who was believing God for several million dollars in his building program. And he was in the church praying about that, "Lord, I need this. I need that." The Lord said, "How would you act if you already had it?" And he said, "I'd be very happy." And then he started praying again, "Oh, Lord, I need the money. Oh, Lord, send the money. Oh, Lord, give us the people. Oh, Lord, make a way. Open a door." God said again to him, "How would you act if you already had it?" He said, "I'd be really happy." Then he started praying again, "Oh, Lord, send the money. Oh, Lord, send the money. Oh, Lord, I've got to have it. Oh, Lord, you said...." Then God interrupted again and said, "How would you act if you already had it?" He said, "I'd be very happy." And God said, "*Well?*"

And then he got the message. He said he started running around his church by himself. He said he started running around that church, jumping up and down, shouting and hollering hallelujah, praising God. He was acting as if he already had what he needed because God was on his side, and the money was on the way! And he said it was just a few months that the money came in to finish the building.

How would you act if you had what you were already believing God for? The victory is ours. There's no confidence in the flesh for righteousness. Our righteousness comes from God as a gift. And in the midst of the trial, it does not change who you are. You can rejoice as an heir of God and a joint-heir with Christ.

Notice it says, "*If so be that we suffer with him, that we may be also glorified together.*" When it says, "suffer with," that doesn't mean sickness and disease, poverty and lack, although there may be sickness trying to attack your body. Or somebody who just says, "Well, I'm just suffering for Jesus." Now, wait a minute; Christ suffered for you. Why would you have to suffer for Him?

But we do suffer temptation. We do suffer tests and trials. We do suffer confrontations of a different sort. But we can focus on

Jesus in the midst of those trials. As a matter of fact, the Bible says to count them all joy (James 1:2). What does that mean? That means we rejoice in the Lord in the midst of the trial because He has overcome for us. I'm getting happy just thinking about it! We are His children and the sheep of His pasture (Psalm 100:3).

RIGHTEOUSNESS IS IN AND ON YOU

Let's look a little closer at righteousness in the relationship to what covenant people do. They worship God in the Spirit, any place, any time, and all the time. They rejoice in Christ Jesus all the time. They're expecting good, great things from a good God. And they have no confidence in the flesh for their righteousness because they're looking to Christ.

Look at this Scripture, Romans 3:21. It says, "*But now the righteousness of God without the law is manifested, being witnessed by the law and the prophets; Even the righteousness of God which is by faith of Jesus Christ unto all and upon all them that believe: for there is no difference.*" So he said something's happened in the New Covenant. Something's happened in Christ. There's been a righteousness revealed that can be seen; it's manifested. It can be seen on you and in you. Righteousness gets in you. Righteousness gets on you. And he said it is ours today through faith in Jesus.

When we talk about being the righteousness of God in Christ, we're bragging on *Jesus*. He said this righteousness comes only by faith in Jesus (or this translation says, it's the faith *of* Jesus, Romans 3:22). We do have the faith of Christ. The same faith He had is in us, and our faith is in Him.

And this righteousness is by Him, comes through Him, and it's in us. It's something that we are, and it's something that we wear.

As a matter of fact, the Bible calls it the robe of righteousness. It's like something gets on you, something gets in you, something starts working for you. Something starts changing your attitude, something starts nudging you to rejoice even in the midnight hour. Don't give up. Don't look down. Don't be dead. Rise up and begin to say, "I'm the righteousness of God in Christ, and I just think I'll get happy right now!" That's a reason to rejoice! I tell you, if there was a reason to rejoice, it's over righteousness because righteousness could never be obtained without Jesus. You could work your fingers to the bone, and you'd never be righteous as Jesus made you righteous through His blood.

So the Bible says in Romans 3:23-24, "*For all have sinned, and come short of the glory of God; Being justified freely by his grace through the redemption that is in Christ Jesus.*" He said, "Look, we know everybody's sinned." That verse is quoted a lot! All have sinned. But listen, the next verse says, "All are justified." The understood subject is *all*. All are justified freely. It didn't cost you anything. It cost God everything, so it's very precious. You might as well wear it. Don't you throw that robe of righteousness into the corner. Get it out, put it on. Wear it. Praise the Lord in it! Rejoice in it! You've been justified freely by His grace through the redemption that is in Christ Jesus. By His grace we are justified. Halleluiah!

Grace, remember, is God's divine "want-to." He declared us righteous in Christ. He made a way for us to be righteous in Christ because He wanted to. He gave His Son for our sin because He wanted to. He loved us. His grace came through for us, and now we are redeemed in Christ freely by His grace.

The Bible says in Romans 8:25, "*Whom* ["whom" is Jesus] *God hath set forth to be a propitiation through faith in his blood.*" Jesus is the one whom God set forth for all to see. I like to say that this was not a private justification. This was not a private righteousness declared upon you. This was a public declaration for everybody to see. For anybody who has faith in My Son, God says, "I declare them righteous publicly. I want the world to know they've been made righteous by the blood of my son. I love them. They love me. I'm on their side. I'm with them."

It is a public declaration of His righteousness. And if God declared it publicly, then *you* should declare it publicly. That doesn't mean you go around telling everybody, "I'm the righteousness of God. I'm the righteousness of God." But you should say it to yourself. You should acknowledge it on a regular basis. It is really one of the core new creation realities of the New Testament. We have been declared the righteousness of God by God in Christ. That understanding begins to open up everything else because righteousness in Christ gives me access to everything Christ has. I'm not an outsider—no, no, no. I'm an *insider*. I am the righteousness of God in Christ. I've become a family member. And it was done for all to see.

If anyone who believes in Jesus is declared righteous by God, we might want to be careful what we say about others. We just might want to be careful how we criticize others. If God has declared them righteous, who are we to judge them? Who are we to condemn them? No. God doesn't want us to criticize others. He wants us to pray for people. He wants us to lift people. He wants us to walk in our redemption and believe the best of others. If He's justified them, we ought to just keep quiet and not criticize them.

It says here that the Lord set Jesus forth as a display of public acceptance of anyone who believes, and that Christ became the propitiation through faith in His blood.

I love to sing songs about the blood. *There Is Power in the Blood.* I frequently sing those old songs in my private devotional time a lot. I like to sing songs about the blood of Jesus because **faith in the blood gives us access to the righteousness of God, and the righteousness of God gives us access to everything God has.** I belong in the family because of the blood. He is the propitiation. We don't use that word "propitiation." I didn't know what it meant until I read it and looked it up in the Bible. It really means "one who restores favor." Christ was set forth on the cross as the One who restores to us the favor of God when we believe in Him. It also means "one who reconnects us to God." I like that definition. He reconnects us to God. And I really like this one: Jesus is the bridge. He bridged the gap between fallen man and a righteous God through His death on the cross. He shed His blood. He's the gap-filler! He restores favor. He reconnects us to God. Thank God, He's still the sweetest name I know. He keeps me singing as I go. He fills my every longing of my heart, keeps me singing as I go. Hallelujah! I can rejoice in Jesus. He's the gap-filler. He's the bridge over troubled waters. He's the bridge that bridges the gap between fallen man and a righteous God. He's the One who restored God's favor. He restored me to God's favor. He's the One who gives me access to all that's in the Kingdom. Jesus, Jesus, sweetest Name I know. He's the One who connects me to God. I'm connected. I've got friends in high places. Have you got One?

ARE YOU CONNECTED?

What happens when you have a bad connection? And when you don't have a good connection, what happens? Things get fuzzy. You can't hear clearly when you don't have a good connection. I go some places, and I can't get any bars on my phone. I don't have a connection! And then all of a sudden it flashes, "No service." People panic when they don't have service. But let me tell you something—God can hear you. And you can hear Him when you are aware of the new creation realities in Christ.

When you and I take time to acknowledge every good thing that's in us in Christ, we have plenty of connection. We've got full bars on our connecting device. We've got that full connection in our heart. We're talking to God. God's talking to us. We're loving one another. We're loving God. We're lifting people. We are connected in Christ. That's called living righteousness as a reality. And it comes from knowing what Jesus did and who He is.

God reconnected us through Christ and through faith in His blood. He declares us righteous openly. God is not ashamed of you. Don't you be ashamed of Him. God declares you righteous openly. And you and I can openly decree our faith in Jesus—not arrogantly, but openly in love knowing that we are in union with Christ. In Christ we have been identified with Him. We have been united to Him. We are declared the righteousness of God in Christ—right with God, free, forgiven, innocent, a new man, a new woman—by God Himself. Hallelujah!

We've got God's best and God's blessing, and God's got our back. So stay on track. Don't look back. There ain't gonna be no lack. Stay on track in righteousness. The blessing of the Lord is yours today in Christ, in every way. So, rise up and dare to say, "I'm the righteousness of God in Christ. That's who I am. That's what I have." God says so. If God says so, it must be so. So I say it like this: "Who said so? God, that's who. I'm not trusting in you. I'm trusting in the Lord. In His Word, in His blood, that's enough for me. I'm free to be all He's called me to be. Righteous and redeemed, that's me.

JUSTIFIED RIGHTEOUS

Look at Romans 5:1, which says, "*Therefore being justified by faith....*" The word "justified," by the way, is the same word translated "righteous," being declared righteous. Somebody said, "Justified means God treats me just as if I'd never sinned. He sees your slate totally clean because of the blood of Jesus. "*Therefore being justified by faith, we have peace with God through our Lord Jesus Christ.*"

Do you see that word *being*? **Our justification, our righteousness is a state of being.** It's not based on actions; it's based on God's grace and a gift in Christ. Now there are good works; I understand that, but we do not do good works in order to be righteous. Righteousness is a gift that comes by faith in Jesus Christ. It's a state of being. It's a divine condition, divinely granted by God. Through faith in Jesus, by faith, we have been declared righteous. And because of that, we have peace with God.

God's on your side. God's for us, not against us. God's not our enemy. He loves us. He's not causing your problems. They blame all kinds of stuff on God. God's not killing people and destroying lives. He loves us. The enemy comes to steal, kill, and destroy. Jesus came that we might have life and have it more abundantly.

So by faith in Jesus we're declared righteous. We have peace with God through our Lord Jesus Christ. God is not our enemy. Therefore, we can boldly proclaim His goodness and His grace over our lives. Well, in order to understand this "therefore" here in chapter 5:1, we need to back up a few verses and see why that "therefore" is there for. Look at what chapter 4:22 says about Abraham: "*And therefore it was imputed to him for righteousness*" (Romans 4:22). What was imputed to him? His faith.

Paul goes on to say, "*Now it was not written for his sake alone, that it was imputed to him; But for us also, to whom it shall be imputed, if we believe on him that raised up Jesus our Lord from the dead; Who was delivered for our offences, and was raised again for our justification*" (Romans 4:23-25).

The word "impute" means to be granted, or as I like to say, divinely given. It was divinely given to Abraham because of his faith. And it says because of our faith in Jesus, it is divinely given to us as well!

Well, here's something I think that needs to be understood. Yes, it is divinely given to us, but it is more than just divinely granted to us. It is actually divinely imparted to us in the new birth. So it's divinely granted, but it's divinely given because the gene of His righteousness is mine through the new birth. I'm born of God. What's in Him got in me.

It's just like my dad in the natural; his genes are in me. I look like him and act like him. I can't help myself because I was in him; now he's in me. Well, that's what's happens in God. We look like God when we start acknowledging and believing and speaking who we are in Christ; then that divine gene of righteousness that's in us goes to work because we begin to understand, "I'm in Him; He's in me. I can't help myself. I just act like Jesus."

TRASH THE PAST

So get over the lies of the enemy! Get over all that condemnation! Put that stuff behind you. Get it where it needs to be. Get it under your feet. Get over the mistakes you've made. We've all made some mistakes. It's time to rise up in the righteousness of God and rejoice in the Lord always, and again I say rejoice. Hallelujah! Get your dance on! Get your praise on! You've got right standing with

God today. You've got total access to all that God has. You have security clearance. You have new creation realities working in you now. Rise up and boldly say, "That's who I am. That's what I have. Everything's gonna be alright!" Hallelujah! Glory be to God! I'm the righteousness of God in Christ.

Paul says this, "*By whom* [Jesus] *also we have access by faith into this grace wherein we stand*" (Romans 5:2, brackets TM). I love that verse, don't you? In Christ I've got total access to everything He has, everything He's done. I'm just not a hobo! I've got access! I've got riches untold in my life. I've got victory. My God, He put something on deposit for me.

You know, I heard a story of a guy there in Chicago. They saw him every day digging in the trash can. Living out of the trash can. Eventually, he died, and they went to his little apartment. When they opened the bed, they found thousands and thousands and thousands of dollars stuffed between the mattresses. And he was living out of the trashcan and sleeping on all of that money. I tell you, you can't live out of the trashcan of life in your mind—the trash of the past.

A lot of people are living in trash of the past when Jesus has made a deposit of forgiveness. Just go ahead and access what He has put on deposit. Begin to acknowledge every good thing that's in you in Christ. And let the communication of your faith become effectual. Hallelujah!

It's like the Bible says in our core verse 2 Corinthians 5:17, "Therefore if any man be in Christ, *let him be* a new creature" (paraphrase). Let it happen! As you acknowledge it, it will overtake you. It will change everything. You can get over the mistakes you've made.

The Lord said to me one time, "Did you ever notice that I did not say every good thing you do will prosper?"

I said, "I didn't notice that." He took me back to Psalm one and it says, "*Everything he doeth shall prosper.*" And he said to me, "I can even make your *mistakes* prosper if you'll keep your heart right."

I said, "Oh, thank you, Jesus!" Because I've made some mistakes! Have you ever made some? I didn't make them on purpose, but we make some mistakes in this life. He can make them prosper if we keep our hearts right. We can rejoice in Christ day in and day out because we have total access. We have security clearance. We have access by faith into this grace wherein we stand. It's like we're standing in a sea of God's great grace, or a sea of God's great righteousness. We've been reclassified, totally qualified, declared righteous by God. The divine gene of righteousness is in me. I'm a partaker of the divine nature in Christ Jesus. Hallelujah! That's a reason to rejoice.

I think it's time for the Church to dance a little bit. I think it's time for us to act free because we are free. Hallelujah! Praise God! There's no sense in acting like the devil. We're just to act like Jesus Christ. We've been redeemed, restored, and reborn by the power of the cross. We've got a reason to get happy! And we can dance our way to victory.

Paul said you're in the middle of God's great ocean of grace, an ocean of God's provision, and an ocean of righteousness—and notice, he said you stand there and *rejoice*! Romans 5:2 tells us, "*By whom also we have access by faith into this grace wherein we stand, and* ***rejoice***."

Rejoicing even in the middle of trials is a mark of your Christianity. The joy of the Lord is your strength. Rejoicing in the Lord is your strength. You've got something to get happy about! You rejoice in hope of the glory of God. Hallelujah! There's always hope in God. The God of hope will grant you all joy and peace in believing, that you may abound in hope, through the power of the Holy Ghost (Romans 15:13 paraphrase).

God is a God of hope! Hallelujah! We've got a reason to rejoice. God is on our side. The blood has been applied. Nothing shall be denied. Every need is supplied. We have the victory! And we can stand in the middle of God's great grace and rejoice in Him in hope of the glory of God. And not only that, but verse three says, "*And not only then, but we rejoice in tribulation*" (Romans 5:3, paraphrased).

Somebody said, "There's two times you ought to rejoice: when you feel like it and when you don't feel like it." And that's right. We rejoice in the good times because we are free. We rejoice in the difficult times because we are free. As a matter of fact, when we learn to rejoice in tribulation, that verse says tribulation will work for us a thing called *patience*. "Patience" the Greek word "hupomoné." The Bible says through patience and faith we inherit the promises of God (Hebrews 6:12). Something good is coming your way. You've been guaranteed the victory, so you might as well rejoice today.

Next it says if you'll let patience work in you, you'll get some experience. And experience will produce hope. Because if God delivered you last time, you'll be delivered this time. If He delivered you before, He'll deliver you again. He's a God that *has* delivered. He's the God that *does* deliver. He's the God that *will* deliver. You might as well rejoice about it!

You've got to get some experience. There are people wanting big money in the job .narket today with no experience. I'm telling you, experience is important. When you experience the delivering power of God, you experience the love of God, you experience the grace of God, you experience the healing hand of God, and you let joy just come forth and you experience victory in God, there's nothing like it! You can just start laughing right in the midst of the storm because you know God's love is shed abroad in your heart. And because of that love that's in Christ Jesus, you always walk in victory! Glory be to God! Hallelujah! The devil can't stop you. You are full of God's mercy, and full of God's grace. You are winning in Christ every day. Romans five tells us that nothing can defeat us if we will set our eyes on Jesus.

And then Paul ends it in verse 17. It says this, "*Those who receive the overflowing gift of grace and of the gift of righteousness shall reign in life by one, Jesus Christ*" (Romans 5:17, paraphrased). I'm reigning in Christ today. I have the victory in every way. I've been made the righteousness of God, you see. Jesus always gives me the victory. Look out, devil, I'm coming through, and there's nothing that you can do! I'm more than a conqueror in Christ. By His power, His grace, and His sacrifice, I'm conformed to His image. That's what I see when I look in the mirror of the Word. Jesus Christ is living in me! Hallelujah! Rejoice in the Lord always, and again I say rejoice!

You are in Him made full, so let it be seen in you today. Rejoice in the Lord in every way—you can, because you are living in Christ.

CHAPTER 7:

FIRST-CLASS FREEDOM

Praise the Lord! Hallelujah! Thank You, Jesus! Amen! I want to open this chapter with the eighth chapter of the Gospel of John because we are going to be looking at our freedom *in Christ.* Do you know that's the only place that real freedom is? Total freedom is in Christ Jesus.

I did a message one time called *First-class freedom* upon which this chapter is based, and that came to me because the freedom we have in Christ is definitely first-class freedom. In other words, there's nothing better. We've got the best, better than all the rest, in Christ. And it can permeate and penetrate every aspect of our lives. Certainly, we know spiritual freedom, but emotional freedom, physical freedom, financial freedom, and relational freedom are a part of that as well. The Bible describes this new creation reality in Christ as the "*good life which God prearranged and made ready for us to live*" (Ephesians 2:10 AMPC).

So when we say first-class freedom, or freedom in Christ, we're talking about freedom from every encumbrance, every hindrance of the enemy, or any difficulty that life can bring our way. Greater is He that's in us than He that's in the world. Christ in you, the Greater One, will put you over.

I like to say this: It's time for all believers to upgrade to first-class freedom. I don't know if you've ever ridden first class on an airline, but I'm telling you, it's a lot better than coach, particularly if you're flying a long way—and I've flown a lot of miles. I've been over in Southeast Asia twenty-five times, so you know that's a lot of miles across that ocean. And I've ridden in coach, and I've ridden first class, or business class, and first class is a lot better.

Let's begin with John 8:30, which says, "*As he spake these words many believed on him. Then said Jesus to those Jews which believed on him....*" If He said it to them then, He's saying it to us now because they believed on Him then. We believe on Him now. That's what you're doing in reading this book on *Living in Christ*—it is because you believe in Jesus. Jesus said to those, or He said to us, "*If ye continue in my word, then are ye my disciples indeed; And ye shall know the truth, and the truth shall make you free*" (John 8:31-32). Praise God! And by the way, that is the first-class freedom that only the truth of the Word of God can bring.

So, there is something interesting about that. He said if you *continue* in my Word. So, really, we don't get it all at one time. The potential is in there, in us—we're perfect in Christ. We've got all things necessary for godliness and to grow into a full man in Christ, or full woman in Christ, totally mature, walking in these new creation realities, but the revelation comes a bit at a time, a step at a time, and from glory to glory.

Jesus said we must continue in the Word if we're going to grow in the Word. I find that to be really a major problem in people's lives sometimes. They get born again. They have a real experience. Christ is their Lord and still is, but they haven't grown spiritually.

And the reason is they haven't continued in the Word. They've been distracted by whatever and not plugged in somewhere where they're getting the Word, not developing a personal relationship with the Lord on a regular basis, and they don't grow. And so continuing in the Word is important even after accepting Jesus, even after reading this book. Don't stop feeding upon the Word of God, because you'll come to know Him in a deeper, richer way than ever before. We just keep going, keep growing, keep showing, and keep knowing.

So He said, "*Continue in my Word*" (John 8:31). And then He said, "*You'll be my disciples indeed*" (verse 31, paraphrased). And remember **the word "disciple" there doesn't just mean a follower of Christ; it means an imitator of Christ.** We're to act like Him. Start looking like Him, thinking like Him, and walking like Him while we're on planet earth. And you shall know the truth and the truth shall make you free.

Revelation is progressive. We stay in it. We stay with it. That's why we're using Philemon the sixth verse that says, "*The communication of our faith becomes effectual as we acknowledge every good thing in us*" (paraphrased) in the new creation realities. So we acknowledge who we are in Christ. We acknowledge who Christ is in us. We feed our faith, starve our doubts to death, and we keep growing in God.

STICK WITH IT

Spiritual strength is defined as consistency of action. I thought that was an incredible definition when I heard it years ago—that if I'll just be consistent I can be strong in the Lord. You may not be able to spend every day, all day, or many hours every day, but you can spend some consistent time with God even when you have a busy life. You can still grow in the knowledge of God.

The Bible said those who practice faith and patience inherit the promises of God (Hebrews 6:12). So one of the meanings for patience is this: just stick with it! Literally, it means to be consistent under pressure. So when Jesus said if you continue in my Word, you'll be My disciples indeed; and you shall know the truth, and the truth shall make you free (John 8:31-32), He knew there would be some pressure, some problems, and some circumstances. And He was saying, "Just continue. Just stick with it, and you'll know the truth, and the truth will set you free."

So somebody says, "Well, the truth makes us free." It's really the truth that we *know* that makes us free! Praise the Lord! Hallelujah! It's that truth that we know because we've spent time with God in the Word. The Holy Spirit is helping us. The Holy Spirit is teaching us. We're spending time fellowshipping with believers. We're hearing the Word in our local church. We're growing in God! We're getting bigger on the inside than we are on the outside.

So even though in the world you have some pressure, don't be surprised by that. Just stay steady. Keep looking to the Lord. Get your mouth to moving. What I mean by that is to speak the Word of God. Acknowledge His grace, His goodness, His ability. Acknowledge your faith in Him and your faith in Christ. And the Bible says we have a victory guarantee. That's pretty good, right?

So let's look at John 16:33. Now, we've looked at this verse before, but I want us to read it so that you can make note of it not just in this book but on your device or in your Bible or in your notes. "*These things I have spoken unto you, that in me ye might have peace.*" Boy, that's powerful, isn't it? That's a great *in Him* verse. **I have peace in Christ.** But notice that that peace was directly related to the Word, to the words Jesus spoke, to the things God said. God's Word produces peace in our lives. We can have peace in the time of trouble. Peace in the midst of the storm. Peace when the winds are raging in the shelter of His arms, in the power of His Word, in the power of who we are in Christ.

"In me ye might have peace," Jesus said, "through My Word. In the world...." If you're in the world, you're going to have trouble. You'll have some trouble, some temptation, some tribulation. But we don't focus on that. Hey, it's going to come, but the victory is ours! The victory is guaranteed. Focus on *Jesus*! Always view the problem from the victory side of the problem, not the problem side of the problem. This is how we handle troubles: Step over through the blood of Jesus to the victory side, look at the problem through the eyes of faith, and begin to decree and declare and acknowledge who you are in Christ.

He said in the world you'll have tribulation, but be of good cheer. I have overcome the world for you. I like a good cheer! When I was playing in basketball, the cheers would encourage me: "Hit 'em in the backbone! Sock 'em in the jaw! Put 'em in the cemetery! Rah, rah, rah!" The point is sometimes you can't get anybody to cheer you on.

But let me tell you something, the Holy Spirit will always cheer you on. David had to encourage himself in the Lord. Well, what does that mean? Well, that means just start thinking about who Christ is, what Jesus did, who you are in Him, and begin to acknowledge some of these Scriptures we've been studying. I'm telling you, as you do that, circumstances change. Your perspective will change. And you'll start viewing the problem from the victory side of the problem. Jesus overcame the world, the flesh, and the devil. Praise God! The devil's got no right to hold us bound or pull us down. We are not going down; we're going over because we are victorious in Christ Jesus.

The Bible said in 2 Corinthians 2:14, *"Now thanks be unto God, which always causeth us to triumph in Christ."* That's a marvelous new creation reality Scripture. There's victory in the new creation. And God causes us to triumph. That says to me that God gets involved in that situation. "He causes us," that means He's getting involved. Some way, somehow He's working behind the scenes for us. Hallelujah! God is on our side. God is for us, not against us.

So in the time of trouble, remember God never sleeps. God never slumbers. So go to bed and rest and worship God when you get up knowing that He's working on the case because of who you are in Christ. Because you've acknowledged His Word, He will bring it to pass. So I tell people, just get with it. Act like the Bible's true. Don't be moping around and wondering how, when, or where God's going to come through. Put your focus on Him and what He's already done for you!

Now listen, challenges come to all of us, and sometimes you take a few moments to adjust and process what's going on—that's normal. But remember the Word and get with it. Let your praise come out. Let your faith dominate because Jesus said we win! Hallelujah!

NO MORE BONDAGE

So in John chapter eight He said, "*You shall know the truth, and the truth shall make you free*" (verse 32). So it's not just the truth. Thank God for the truth, but it's the truth we know that makes us free.

Well, the guys He was talking to said, "*What do you mean free? We've never been in bondage*" (John 8:33, paraphrased).

Jesus said to them, "*If you are a servant of sin, if you haven't been freed from sin's dominion, you are in bondage and don't even know it*" (John 8:34, paraphrased). And then He quoted verse 36. Boy, do we love this Scripture. It says this: "*If the Son therefore shall make you free, ye shall be free indeed.*"

Now that is a first-class freedom. Only Jesus can give a first-class freedom. Some people think money is freedom. And that's good; we need some provision. But listen, freedom goes beyond that. Freedom starts in our spirit, radiates to our soul, gets in our body, gets in our circumstance, gets in our family. Praise God! It's a freedom that only Jesus can give. You can't get free from sin any other way except through Christ. You can have a lot of things in life, but if you're not free from sin, what does it profit you if you gain the whole world and lose your soul (Mark 8:36)? Remember 1 Corinthians 15:22, "*In Adam all die, in Christ all are made alive.*" So you're either in Adam in sin, or you're in Christ in the gift of righteousness. And the only way to get there is by faith in Jesus.

I have a song that says:

I'm free from sin, say it over again.
I'm free from sin indeed.
No evil thing can come again
And lord it over me.
Since Jesus died, was crucified upon that cruel tree.
And by His blood He brought me life,
And from sin set me free.

Then it goes:

And there is therefore now no condemnation
Living here in me.
For I walk not after the law of sin and death,
But the law of liberty.
Oh, I'm free from sin
Say it over again.
I'm free from sin indeed.
No evil thing can come again
And lord it over me.
Since Jesus died, was crucified upon that cruel tree
And by His blood He brought me life
And from sin set me free.

Praise God! Now that is an in Christ reality. That is a new creation reality. And that is a great song to reinforce your faith in Jesus, acknowledging the good thing that He's done in you and that freedom is ours simply by receiving Jesus and acknowledging His goodness and His grace. And the law of the Spirit of life in Christ begins to go to work to bring to us a first-class freedom. That is what it means to be living in Christ.

DEAD TO SIN

Now let's check out Romans chapter six. I want to just wade down through this chapter a little bit because this is a chapter of freedom because of Christ. So let's just simply start in verse one, and we'll read a few Scriptures and handpick a few.

Romans 6:1-2 says, "*What shall we say then? Shall we continue in sin, that grace may abound? God forbid. How shall we, that are dead to sin, live any longer therein?*" We have been reclassified in Christ. We've been called sons and daughters of God. Our sins have been not just covered but remitted, washed away, gone! We are now redeemed by the blood of Jesus. And the Bible uses the term "we are dead to sin" and all of its effects.

Well, does that mean I don't ever make a mistake? No, it doesn't mean that. What it does mean is that when you make a mistake, you receive forgiveness because forgiveness is yours through the blood of Jesus. Don't stay in the sin, and don't beat yourself up, and don't stay down in the "stumble," as I like to say to people. Go forward because Christ is in you.

Verses 3-4 say, "*Know ye not, that so many of us as were baptized into Jesus Christ were baptized into his death? Therefore we are buried with him by baptism into death: that like as Christ was raised up from the dead by the glory of the Father, **even so we also**....*" Man, do I love those words together! "***Even so we also** should walk in newness of life.*" Sometimes I just take the "w" off the "we" and replace it with an "m" and I say, "Even so, *me* also!" What does that mean? Well, just as Jesus was crucified, we died with Him. Just as Christ was raised from the dead, we were raised with Him. Praise God, that's my new identity. I'm identified in His death, burial, and resurrection. I'm identified in His seating in heavenly places. I'm identified with His victory. We are in Christ. And it says very plainly that just like God raised Jesus from the dead by His glory, by His power, by His might, even so we also have been raised from the dead. And because we've been raised from the dead by the power of God, we can walk in newness of *zoe*, life, God-life! Praise God! Hallelujah!

This makes the devil nervous. He doesn't want us finding out what happened when Jesus rose from the dead and how it affected us today. The same power that raised Christ from the dead raised us up to this new creation in Christ Jesus (Romans 8:11). And I have *newness*—I love that word—newness of life in Christ. That's who I am—and that's who you are!

So, for instance when symptoms try to come against our body, we understand that healing is part of our redemption in Christ. The Bible said He was wounded, He was bruised, and by His stripes we're healed (Isaiah 53:5). But you've got to fight the good fight of faith. How do you fight the good fight of faith? By speaking the Word, because faith comes by hearing, and hearing by the Word of God. The life of God in me quickens my mortal body, and this sickness, this disease, and any symptoms have to depart in Jesus' name. And then begin to praise the Lord and thank the Lord.

You say, "Will they leave right away?" Probably not, but they could. But in the process of your faith working and you acknowledging every good thing that's in you in Christ, you better know that the disease has been defeated, and it will depart from your body, and you'll walk in the power of the resurrection, the name of Jesus, the blood of the Lamb, and help that is ours in Christ. Praise God!

So it does take patience, consistency, and faith. It takes speaking God's Word, walking in God's love, and letting Him perform that. And it may take a little while, but I tell you what, it's working. Just rebuke that devil, and rebuke those symptoms, and claim your healing in Jesus' mighty name.

There's something about revelation in Christ that frees me from the law of sin and death. The law of sin and death does not belong to me. Disease is not mine. Confusion is not mine. Jesus came that

I might be made whole spirit, body, and soul. Hallelujah! I am free in Christ. I've got a first-class freedom. Hallelujah!

SAY GOODBYE TO THE OLD MAN

OK, look at Romans 6:5 "*For if we have been planted together in the likeness of his death, we shall be* [raised] *also in the likeness of his resurrection*" (brackets TM). We get baptized in water as a sign and a symbol of our faith in Christ—we're buried and raised. But He said, this really happened to your *spirit man*. You were crucified with Christ. You've been raised with Christ.

Verse six says, "*Knowing this, that our old man is crucified with him....*" Our old man is crucified with him. Now, that's not talking about your dad. (Some people call their dad, "My old man." I would never call my dad my "old man" because I have too much respect for my dad.) This old man is the old *you* that's been crucified with Christ, the old sinful nature. A new man has been resurrected.

My dad lost both of his hands before I was born. He was a young, twenty-two-year-old father. His right arm was cut off between the wrist and the elbow, and on his left hand, all four fingers were missing. So I only knew my dad with a thumb. And do you know, God called him to preach. He designed and invented tools. He designed a hammer that fit on his nub, and he actually became a pioneer pastor. He built some of the parsonages that we lived in—remodeled the churches that he pastored. He pastored *fifty* years. So, I'm just saying all things are possible to those who believe. My dad could play guitar with no hands. He designed tools! He could play Hawaiian style.

Your "old man" is not somebody related to you; it's *you*. The old man that you were in your sinful state, was crucified with Christ. There's that "with" identification.

Go back to verse 6: "*Knowing this, that our old man is crucified with him, that the body of sin might be destroyed, that henceforth we should not serve sin*" (Romans 6:6). The devil is a liar! Anything he's tried to do to you, Christ has *undone*, and the victory is ours! We start claiming this first-class freedom in Christ based on this Scripture, and the sins that would try to dominate us will dominate us no more.

Verse seven says, "*For he that is dead is freed from sin.*" Hallelujah! Verse eight: "*Now if we be dead with Christ, we believe that we shall also live with him.*" I believe it, don't you? I'm alive unto God. I'm dead to sin. I'm dead to this world. I'm dead to the dominion of darkness, and I'm alive unto God. Hallelujah! Praise the Lord! Glory to God!

And as we acknowledge that, then the reality of that comes forth because it's real in my spirit, in your spirit. But it begins to come forth and dominate the way we think and the way we act and what we do.

"*Knowing that Christ being raised from the dead dieth no more; death hath no more dominion over him*" (verse 9). I think we can say death has no more dominion over me. If I'm in Christ, I get what He got. So I acknowledge that.

This is a bold statement. What does it mean? Does it mean you're never going to leave this body and die? No, but when you do leave this body, to be absent from the body is to be present with the Lord. You and I as Christians, believers, are alive forevermore. Never taste death! No way! That's worth praising God over!

THE DEVIL IS A DEFEATED FOE

I'll tell you this, the devil just can't kill you whenever he wants to. He wouldn't let you read this book. He's not this all-powerful being that he acts like he is. He is a defeated foe through the blood of Jesus, and you have dominion over him in Jesus' name. And you can rise up and decree darkness has no more dominion over me. Death has no more dominion over me. No devil has dominion over me. Praise God, I'm free from poverty, sickness, and death in Christ. Hallelujah! Amen! Glory to God! Those are acknowledgments, declarations, statements of faith that create the realities that are ours in the realm of the spirit.

Let's continue looking at Romans 6:9: "*Knowing that Christ being raised from the dead dieth no more; death hath no more dominion over him.*"

It's wonderful to know that Jesus destroyed the power of the enemy, and He destroyed the power of death and redeemed people—you and I and everyone who will dare to believe—from the fear of death.

Did you know they say that the number one fear, the mother of all fears, is the fear of death? There are hundreds of phobias, and we could talk about those, but we don't need to. Out of all of those phobias people deal with, everything from being afraid of heights, being afraid of the dark, being afraid of dogs, being afraid of peanut butter getting stuck to the roof of your mouth (there's a real phobia of that!) the mother of all phobias is the fear of death. And Jesus came to deliver us from that.

We'll come back to Romans six, but there is another important Scripture that is worth the detour. Hebrews 2:14 says, "*Forasmuch then as the children are partakers of flesh and blood, he also himself* [Jesus, Son of God, God in the flesh] *likewise took part of the same*" (brackets TM). He became a man born of a woman, born under the law, and He redeemed us as God's great substitute for our sins. It goes on to say, "*That through death he* [Jesus] *might destroy him that had the power of death, that is, the devil*" (brackets TM).

The devil thought he was getting rid of Jesus, but really Jesus was getting rid of him—defeating him. The devil's still around, but to the Christians who know who they are in Christ, the devil is *defeated and powerless.* As a matter of fact, that word *destroy* means "to make of no effect or to bring to naught, to bring to zero, to bring to nothing, or to loose one from the power of." Praise God! Hallelujah!

So, to the believer, the enemy is defeated under our feet, but many believers don't know that.

My dad was a minister for fifty years, and when I began to learn some of these truths about who we are in Christ, I started sharing some with him...and he had never heard that before! But thank God, we know who Jesus is. We're beginning to understand who we are in Him, and the enemy is under our feet.

The Bible said he destroyed him—to bring him to nothing, to break all of his effects, to bring him to naught—"*him that had the power of death, that is the devil; And deliver them who through fear of death were all their lifetime subject to bondage*" (Hebrews 2:14-15).

Praise God! The fear of death is broken! It has no more dominion over me. All fears are broken. God did not give us the spirit of fear, but of power, love, and a sound mind. Jesus came to accomplish that in His death, burial, resurrection, and ascension, and we have been raised up to sit with Him in heavenly places. Praise God! Hallelujah!

You have to resist those things that are not of Him that try to come in. Resist doubt. Resist fear. Resist those things in Jesus' name. They have to flee.

Now let's read on. Hebrews 2:16 goes on to say, "*For verily he took not on him the nature of angels* [talking about Jesus]*; but he took on him the* [nature of the] *seed of Abraham*" (brackets TM). He took our sinful nature that we might have His nature. His nature is a righteousness nature, is a love nature, is a God nature. That's what's in us! You talk about freedom! He took on our nature so we could have His nature.

"*Wherefore in all things it behoved him to be made like unto his brethren, that he might be a merciful and faithful high priest in things pertaining to God, to make reconciliation for the sins of the people*" (verse 17). Jesus is our faithful and merciful high priest. What does that mean? That He's always faithful to show you and me mercy. Hallelujah! Come boldly to the throne of grace, that you may obtain mercy, find grace to help in time of need" (Hebrews 4:16, paraphrased).

"*For in that he himself hath suffered being tempted, he is able to succor* [run to the aid of] *them that are tempted*" (Hebrews 2:18, brackets TM). I don't know about you, but I read these verses in light of a first-class freedom and I thought, "*What else could He have ever done for me than what He's already done?*" It is a complete redemption. It is an everlasting release. And He is running toward me today—lifting me, loving me, helping me. Thank you, Jesus. Praise God. Don't you love Him? Hallelujah! The devil is defeated, and our High Priest knows exactly what it is like to be us—and He loves us anyway, all day, every day! Now, wasn't that worth the side trip?

DON'T LET SIN REIGN

Let's go back to Romans chapter six and begin to finish this out. "*Knowing that Christ being raised from the dead dieth no more; death hath no more dominion over him* [or me in Christ]" (Romans 6:9). Boy, that's a good bold statement. Don't be afraid of the devil. He ain't nothin' but a hound dog, and he's defeated in Jesus' Name. Be bold to speak who you are in Christ.

"*For in that he died, he died unto sin once: but in that he liveth, he liveth unto God*" (Romans 6:10). Look at verse 11: "*Likewise reckon ye also yourselves....*" "Reckon ye," we don't use that word *reckon* so much. It means, "think of yourself this way." Get this mental picture. Meditate on this statement. "*I am dead unto sin, but I am alive unto God through Jesus Christ my Lord*" (verse 11, paraphrased). There's that little word *through*. Through my faith in Him, through what He did for me, I function in this life. By faith in Christ, I'm alive unto God.

I love the Amplified Bible of that. It says, "*I'm living in unbroken fellowship with God in Christ Jesus*" (Romans 6:11, AMPC paraphrased). Praise God! Hallelujah!

Even when you miss the mark, and maybe fall short, say something you shouldn't say or do something you shouldn't do, it doesn't change your *condition*. You're still the righteousness of God in Christ. And all that unrighteousness can't cling as long as you run to Jesus and let Him run to you. He paid the price for all of our sins once for all time! So let's receive it. Let's believe it. Let's accept it. Let's acknowledge it. Hallelujah! And let's stay free! (1 John 1:9)

Verse 12 says, "*Let not sin therefore reign in your mortal body, that ye should obey it in the lusts thereof.*" So it doesn't say that it's not there or it doesn't want to try to creep in and cause us to stumble. He said, "Don't let it reign." One way we do that is by our revelation of who we are in Christ and acknowledging new creation realities. We're going to let that new creation dominate us. We're not letting the old man dominate us. We're not going to let sin dominate us. We're not going to let the devil dominate us. We're not going to let fear dominate us. Praise God! We have first-class freedom! But we have a part to play. We've got to resist the enemy, and he'll flee. If you don't resist him, then he'll try to hang around and just bug you. But, you can tell him, "Shut up. Get under my feet in Jesus' name." Don't let sin reign.

Romans 6:13 tells us, "*Neither yield ye your members as instruments of unrighteousness unto sin: but yield yourselves unto God, as those that are alive from the dead, and your members as instruments of righteousness unto God.*" The margin says, "And your members as weapons." **Did you know your mouth is a weapon of righteousness?** When you open up and begin to love Jesus, worship Jesus, praise Jesus, and you open up and begin to speak His Word and begin to acknowledge every good thing in you, your mouth becomes a weapon of righteousness!

The devil can't stand it. And he can't withstand it because victory belongs to us in Christ. Your hands can be a weapon of righteousness—lifting your hands to the Lord, clapping your hands in praise and adoration, and reaching your hands out to the lost, the weary, the broken, the needy. He said use your instruments, so use your hands as weapons of righteousness as new creations in Christ.

Verse 14, "*For sin shall not have dominion over you* [me]" (brackets TM). I like to put me in there. I think you ought to put yourself in there too. Sin shall not have dominion over me. There's a lot of sin in this world! Satan's running around seeing whom he may devour, to steal, kill, and destroy—but not you, not me. I'm in Christ. And as I acknowledge who I am in Christ, acknowledge His grace, His love, His mercy, and His power, something takes place that changes everything. I'm not under the law. I'm under grace. And His grace is sufficient for me—and you! Hallelujah! Praise God! Hallelujah!

So don't go back and live under the law. I like to tell people, "Hey, learn from the Old Testament, but live in the New Testament." We're in Christ. We've got a New Covenant. And sin shall not have dominion over us. Sin is broken. But you have to affirm it, believe it, acknowledge it, stand on it. Don't live in guilt and shame. Live in the power of Jesus' name and declare, "I am free from sin and Satan in all of its form and all of its influence. I am the righteousness of God in Christ. I've got a first-class freedom. Jesus is Lord of my life, and He has set me free." Praise God!

Let's jump to Romans 6:22, "*But now being made free from sin* [that's me], *I have become a servant to God. I have my fruit unto holiness, and the end is everlasting zoe*" (paraphrased, brackets TM).

"*For the wages of sin is death; but the gift of God is eternal life through Jesus Christ our Lord*" (verse 23). Hallelujah! You shall know the truth, and the truth shall make you free (John 8:32). We have the gift of God in Christ, and we're not defeated by the enemy anymore. Oh, he may show up, but just slap him down in Jesus' name. Praise God! Don't give him any room. Give no place to him.

Now let's go to Colossians as we wind this chapter up. Colossians chapter one is talking about first-class freedom. Colossians 1:12 says, "*Giving thanks unto the Father, which hath made us meet to be partakers of the inheritance of the saints in light.*"

Now we don't use that term, "which has made us meet." You know, I've never seen that anyplace or used it, but it really means "enabled us" or "qualified us." I like both of those translations. Let's read it that way. "*Giving thanks unto the Father, who has enabled us and qualified us to be partakers of the inheritance of the saints in light, or in Christ*" (paraphrased). Hallelujah!

I have been qualified. I like to say I'm *pre*qualified through the blood of Jesus. I'm not waiting for an answer, like if you're going to buy a house and you've got to go get qualified at the bank. You're waiting for an answer to see if you've qualified. I'm not waiting for an answer. I've got an answer right here. I've got it right here—Colossians 1:12. So don't let the devil disqualify you. Don't let your past disqualify you. Don't let your mistakes disqualify you. Rise up in the light of the love of God and in the light of who Christ is and declare, "I am qualified to partake of my inheritance in Christ." Praise God. Everything Christ has is mine. The Bible calls us heirs of God and joint-heirs with Jesus. That's powerful, isn't it? Praise God! Hallelujah!

Colossians goes on to say, "*Who hath delivered us from the power of darkness, and hath translated us into the kingdom of his dear Son*" (verse 13). I'm delivered from the dominion of darkness of the devil, and I've been translated. I'm not just delivered and left and on my own. I've been delivered from, taken out of, and put into a new Kingdom—the Kingdom of the Son of His love. And remember, there is no lack in the Kingdom. And that's where we are delivered from and brought into. We're looking to the Lord in the Kingdom. Great is our reward in the Kingdom. I'm in the Kingdom! There's victory in the Kingdom. I'm set free in the Kingdom. There is no doubt in the Kingdom. I passed the test; I get God's best in the Kingdom! Praise the Lord! I'm in the Kingdom of His dear Son. That's who I am. I'm walking in light. I'm living by

His power. I'm living by His might. Victory is mine today in every way because I'm in the Kingdom of His dear Son. Hallelujah!

IN WHOM WE HAVE EVERYTHING

Colossians 1:14 finishes with a powerful concept: "*In whom we have redemption through his blood, even the forgiveness of sins.*" The forgiveness of sins, all sins, *all sins*—past, present, future—have been laid upon Jesus. Let go and let God be God.

In a book by E.W. Kenyon I love, there's one chapter entitled *In Whom We Have*. In whom we have what? Well, *everything*! In Him we have everything, but without whom we have nothing when it comes to God-stuff. Jesus is our qualifier. Jesus is our Redeemer.

In the New Testament, that phrase is used several times, "in whom we have." I thought it might be a good assignment for you just to go through some of Paul's letters and look for the things we have. I'll tell you that there are a couple of them in Ephesians. I gave you one for free—"*In whom we have redemption*" (Colossians 1:14). I challenge you to find out what the other two or three say, because that's where we have our redemption. That's where we have all that God has given us in Christ.

We have a first-class freedom. It's yours today. Will you lay hold of it?

CHAPTER 8:

REDEMPTION IN CHRIST

I believe the Holy Spirit is going to work in a mighty way in all of our lives in this chapter. We're trusting Him to reveal to us the truth of who we are in Christ, what Christ has done for us, and these new creation realities.

We're going to begin this chapter in Galatians chapter three, and we're going to this subject: our redemption in Christ. Because of Who He is and what He did, we are redeemed. I am the redeemed of the Lord. You are the redeemed of the Lord through faith in Christ Jesus.

So let's define "redeemed." Redeemed means "to buy back." If you buy back something, you redeem it. Another meaning for redeemed is "to purchase the freedom of." Now certainly that's been done through life and circumstances or situations. You can purchase the freedom of someone, or from something, such as paying off their debt. It means to set free. It means to exchange for better—we have a better covenant in Christ, built on better promises, purchased by better blood.

I added this definition because I wanted to direct our thinking to the heart of God when He sent Christ to redeem us. To redeem would mean "to buy back something that you wanted, that you needed, that you loved, or that you missed." And I believe we qualified in all those categories in the heart of God. He did what He did because He wanted us. He wanted to. He needed our relationship in the sense that God is love, and He could not do without us. Whatever it took, He was willing to pay the price, go the distance to redeem us, even to the sending of His own Son. Hallelujah! Thank you, Jesus. Amen. He loved us. That's why He redeemed us.

The Bible says in order for God "*to satisfy the great and wonderful and intense love*" (Ephesians 2:4, AMPC) that He has for us, He quickened us together in Christ Jesus (paraphrased). In other words, His love could be satisfied no other way than to redeem us from the hand of the enemy.

Galatians 3:13 says, "*Christ hath redeemed us from the curse of the law, being made a curse for us...*" There's that little phrase *for us*. He was made a curse on our behalf. Remember, the revelation of who we are in Christ is tied up in these little prepositions. The new creation realities come alive when we understand the word *for*, the word *by*, the word *through*, the word *with*, and the word *in*.

He did it for us on our behalf, "*...for it is written, Cursed is every one that hangeth on a tree*" (Galatians 3:13). Now when Paul said, "hanged on a tree," that meant the cross. He hung there in our place, became a curse for us with our sin. He was not a sinner, but He was made to *be sin* for us—substitutionary. He took our sickness. He took our pain. He took our grief. He took our sorrow. He took what we were, so we could become as He is. Praise the Lord! Hallelujah! Thank you, Jesus! Amen.

So, He was hanged on a tree, or hung on the cross for our sin, and became a curse for us—separated from God for us so we would never have to be separated again. And look at verse 14, He did all that, "*that the blessing of Abraham might come on the Gentiles*," which is most likely you and me. Anyone outside of the Jewish nation is classified a Gentile, so He said this blessing got bigger than just one nation. In Christ, it went to everybody. Before it was just to one nation—God's people, Israel. But now in Christ everybody gets some.

"*That the blessing of Abraham might come on the Gentiles through Jesus Christ, that we might receive the promise of the Spirit through faith*" (Galatians 3:14). Now there are two words "through" in that verse. *Through* is one of our key prepositions—*through* Christ, *through* faith. And, actually, that's the way everything is received from God—through Christ, through faith. It's because of Jesus and what He did and our faith in that. So Christ redeemed us from the curse of the law, being made a curse for us on our behalf, that the blessing of Abraham might come on the Gentiles through Jesus Christ, that we might receive the promise of the Spirit through faith. Make sense so far?

So something got *on* you when you came to Christ, and something got *in* you when you came to Christ. This is an inside work of the Holy Spirit that affects your life in every way. We have a complete redemption in Christ—spirit, soul, body. It's financially, physically, emotionally, circumstantially, and in our relationships. The blessing of God, which it calls the blessing of Abraham or the blessing of Jesus, has come upon us through faith.

The Holy Spirit is in charge of helping us walk in the reality of that as we get into who we are in Christ, and as we get into the Word, the Holy Spirit begins to unfold it all. He begins to help us come to know in a deeper way who Christ is, what Christ did, and what that means to you and me today. That's why we say, like in Philemon, one of our text Scriptures, that the communication of our faith becomes effectual "as we acknowledge" every good thing that's in us in Christ Jesus. And then we say, "That's who I am, and that's what I have."

HOW WE ARE TO LIVE

Remember, the word "through" means *function.* I think it would be good to define that because I've used it a lot. The word "function" means "a specific action or activity." The way we live, the way we think through Christ, through His death, burial, and resurrection—we're renewing our minds to act and think like God. We take action. We take steps of faith as God is working in our life.

The word "function" not only means that, but it is action and activity that are proper. It's also the purpose in which one is designed for. We are designed to function in the purpose of God on planet earth. We are carrying the hope of Christ to a lost and dying world. We are lifting up the name that's above every name. The Bible says at the mention of that name, every knee shall bow and every tongue will confess that Jesus Christ is Lord.

So our purpose is to function through the reality of what Christ did and what His blood provided. We are to function according to the action and activity that is designed in the Word of God—thinking that way, acting that way, talking that way, living that way, giving that way, working that way, praising that way. The purpose we're designed for in the new creation is to live by faith. What does that mean? That means faith in the promise of God, faith in the Word of God, faith in the blood of Jesus.

So through faith, through the help of the Holy Spirit, and through Christ Jesus, we are blessed. Abraham's blessing was something like this: God said to him, "In blessing, I will bless you." That means blessing upon blessing upon blessing. I will be your God, and you will be My son (or daughter or family). God said, "I will treat you like family." In Christ *we* are family. Hallelujah!

Look at Galatians 3:16: "*Now to Abraham and his seed were the promises made. He saith not, And to seeds, as of many; but as of one, And to thy seed, which is Christ.*" So God told Abraham, "To you and your seed I will be God, I will be a Father. I will bless you. I'll be with you. I'll take your part. I'll be on your side." Praise God. Hallelujah! And that promise was made to Abraham and his seed, meaning *the Seed*, which is Christ, who came according to the prophecy and the Word of God.

We are in the seed—we are in Christ. Therefore, we're in the blessing. Hallelujah The blessing of the Lord has come upon me. I am blessed in Christ. That's who I am. That's what I have.

When I confess this, what am I doing? I'm acknowledging that good thing. And as I acknowledge it, it becomes effectual. I begin to realize the manifestation of it, the working of it, the power of it, the effect of it, and the influence of it in my life because Jesus purchased it for me.

Let's talk a little bit more about the seed. The same chapter, Galatians 3:26, goes on to say, "*For ye are all the children of God by faith in Christ Jesus.*" Well, there you go. That sort of makes it plain, doesn't it? Everybody's a son or daughter of God in Christ Jesus. Remember, in Adam all die, in Christ all are made alive. Well, not only are we made alive, but remember we are really granted and given sonship or the privileges of children, heirs of God and joint-heirs with Christ.

Now, He granted that to us, yes, but it's also inherent in us because we're born of the Spirit of God. Our spirit is born of His

Spirit. And His Spirit lives in our spirit. Because we are connected to God through the new birth and through the power of the Holy Spirit, we can function in life in Christ in the name of Jesus with great hope and great expectation that something good is happening today because of Jesus. We all are the children of God by faith in Christ. We're saved by grace through faith. So faith accesses what grace has provided. And He has provided total redemption, total sonship, total family, and total inheritance in Christ for us. And the more we acknowledge it, the more real it becomes to us. Praise the Lord! Hallelujah! Thank you, Jesus!

TAKE OFF THAT OLD THING

Look at verse 27: "*For as many of you as have been baptized into Christ have put on Christ.*" Now what does that mean? Well, it means that we have put on the new nature of Christ. We are dressed in the robe of righteousness. We are dressed in the helmet of salvation. We are dressed in Christ—through Christ we put Him on. That would indicate to us that **we have taken off the old Adam and put on the new Christ.**

Let's look at that just a moment. We'll come back to Galatians, but we are going to visit Ephesians chapter four to see something important. Ephesians 4:20-22 says this: "*But ye have not so learned Christ; If so be that ye have heard him, and have been taught by him, as the truth is in Jesus: That ye put off concerning the former* [lifestyle] *conversation* [the word conversation means "lifestyle," or] *the old man*" (brackets TM) We put off the old man, and we put on the new man. And the old man is corrupt according to deceitful lusts (verse 22, paraphrased).

So that's the old nature. We're putting on the new nature, which is in Christ. And the more we acknowledge who we are in

Christ, the more of the old man just drops off! He's dead and gone, and he just drops off. But if we never acknowledge who we are in Christ, he likes to hang on and tries to control our life with attitudes and actions and habits and all of that same old stuff to which we are supposed to be dead. "*And be renewed in the spirit of your mind. And that ye put on the new man, which after God is created in righteousness and true holiness*" (Ephesians 4:23-24).

So I want you to focus on putting on the new you, putting on that image of the resurrected Christ that is in us. Acknowledging every good thing that's in you in Christ causes that old nature to just fade away. There's something so powerful about the resurrected Christ that it changes *everything*. You can leave that old you in the grave and live a new life.

He says, "*Put away lying, and be angry and sin not*" (Ephesians 4:25-26, paraphrased). So Paul begins to talk about how the old man operated. Somebody says, "Well, I'm just going to give you a piece of my mind." Well, you better control that, he says, because if you don't, you'll give place to the devil.

The devil's not all powerful, but he is an opportunist. He tries to find an opportunity to steal, kill, and destroy. When we get caught up in who we are in Christ, the old man fades away and never raises his ugly head. Oh, he tries—anger, and attitudes, and hurt feelings, and all that stuff tries to come, but you can remind yourself of who you are in Christ.

Paul says let him that stole, steal no more, but let him work that he may have to give (Ephesians 4:28 paraphrased). We live a life of giving and receiving from God. He said corrupt communication will be done away with when you put on the new (verse 29), and you won't be grieving the Holy Spirit (verse 30). You'll be walking in harmony with the Holy Spirit, because He is helping us put on the new.

Verse 31 says, "*All bitterness, and wrath, and anger, and clamour, and evil speaking, with all malice*" will be done away with when you put on the new you. Hallelujah!

I don't want you to be caught up in bitterness and pain and situations of the past. Those things try to hang on. Some folks have had that stuff hang on for years and years. And it stunts their spiritual growth. But when you learn this truth, that you're a new creature in Christ, old things like that have passed away, and all things have become new, we begin to acknowledge that bitterness is absolutely healed, that anger is done away with, that wrath goes somewhere else! Hallelujah! You rise up in resurrection power, and you do what verse 32 says, and you "*be kind one to another, tenderhearted, forgiving one another, even as God for Christ's sake hath forgiven you.*" That's the new man right there. Be kind! Be tenderhearted. Reach out to people. Forgive people. Praise the Lord! Hallelujah!

And then he said in Ephesians 5:1-2, "*Be ye therefore followers of God, as dear children; And walk in love, as Christ also hath loved us, and hath given himself for us an offering and a sacrifice to God for a sweetsmelling savour.*" So that word "followers" of God means be "imitators" of God. How are we going to imitate God? Through faith, through the help of the Holy Spirit, through new creation realities—that is how we imitate God.

TRY ON YOUR NEW OUTFIT

Now we're going to go back to Galatians 3:27, which says, "*For as many of you as have been baptized into Christ have put on Christ.*" So that's talking about putting on the new man, which I just showed you in Ephesians four. Now look at verse 28: "*There is neither Jew nor Greek, there is neither bond nor free, there is neither male nor female: for ye are all one in Christ Jesus.*" Amen!

Everybody gets the same dose of the Holy Ghost. Everybody gets the same measure of faith. Everybody gets the same deal. It's called the Jesus deal. Praise God. Hallelujah! It's the best deal. And we come to Him as we are, and He makes us as He is, whether you're male or female, Jewish or Gentile. Whatever nationality you may be, it doesn't matter. Wherever you were born, it doesn't matter. You have equal access to God through faith in Christ.

He said in verse 29, "*And if ye be Christ's* [belong to Christ], *then are ye Abraham's seed, and heirs according to the promise*" (brackets TM). Hallelujah! Well, I'm in the seed. His name is Jesus. And He's the one who got the blessing for me. He's the One who secured my redemption. He's the One who set me free. So I like to talk about Jesus, the King of kings, the Lord of lords—supreme, throughout eternity. He's the great I AM; the way, the truth, the life; the door.

So I'm blessed. I'm blessed in the city. I'm blessed in the field. I'm blessed by His power. I'm blessed to do His will. I'm blessed coming in. I'm blessed going out. I'm blessed to be a blessing. I've got a song on one of my CDs called, "I'm blessed." And that's the words to the first verse. The second verse goes:

I'm blessed in my body.
I'm blessed in my mind.
I'm blessed in my money.
I'm blessed all the time.
I'm blessed in the morning.
I'm blessed every night.
I'm blessed to be a blessing.
Everything's gonna be alright
Because I'm blessed.

And we can sing, "*I'm blessed. I'm blessed, blessed. I'm blessed, blessed, blessed*" because of what Jesus has done. We're blessed in Christ with the blessing of Abraham. It really is the blessing of the Seed, who is Jesus. We're blessed in the Seed. We're blessed by God. We are a blessing. Hallelujah! We're free from sin, free from Satan's dominion, free from the curse of the law. We are free from poverty, sickness, death, and demonic oppression. We are free from the works of darkness. We are free from the power of the enemy. We are blood-blessed, blood-bought, and Holy Spirit taught. I'm telling you, you are somebody in Christ!

We're not going to take time to go back and read the curse of the law, but you can find it in Deuteronomy 28. I encourage you to go read it. I like to say something like this: there are sixty-three verses of curses, and none belong to me, for by the blood of Jesus, I am set free. Hallelujah!

When you sum up all those curses, they mean poverty, sickness, and death. We are free from that. That death would mean certainly spiritual death, but I believe it means premature death as well. The devil just can't kill you and me anytime he wants to. I can live long and strong because of the blessing. I'm free from poverty, sickness, and death. That's who I am. That's what I have. And you begin to acknowledge that, it becomes effectual in your life and your circumstances.

GOD'S TRUTH IS: YOU ARE BLESSED!

Let's go to the Old Testament a moment to another verse. We are redeemed from the curse of the law. Numbers 23:19 says, "*God is not a man, that he should lie* [So God's Word is true]*; neither the son of man, that he should repent: hath he said, and shall he not do it? or hath he spoken, and shall he not make it* *good?*" (brackets TM). Hallelujah! God watches over His Word to perform it. He's not a man that He can lie; you can trust Him.

Verse 20 continues, "*Behold, I have received commandment to bless: and he hath blessed; and I cannot reverse it.*"

Now, you can go back and read the whole story. It's a king trying to get one of the prophets to really speak a word against Israel. And the prophet says, "I can't do that. God's blessed them, and I can't reverse that blessing." **Your blessing can't be reversed.** It's in Christ. It's eternal. Just step on into it. By faith, acknowledge it.

I like verse 21, "*He hath not beheld iniquity in Jacob* [me]." I like to put "me" in there, because we've got Scripture for that in Hebrews 10. He does not remember our sins and our iniquities anymore in Christ. So, He has not beheld iniquity in me or you in Christ. Neither has he seen perverseness in me or you. He sees us in Christ. God is with us, and the shout of a king is among us (verse 21, paraphrased). Hallelujah! Praise the Lord! Sometimes I just like to shout when I read things like that, and you should too! Rejoice by faith because God's with you. He's not looking at any of our sins. He doesn't even remember them anymore! The blood of Jesus has set us free.

Look at verse 22, "*God brought* [me] *them out of Egypt*" (brackets TM). Egypt stands for the land of bondage. One person said it means the land of limitation where you are bound and hindered and not part of the covenants of God. But now, in Christ, you are His covenant people and the sheep of His pasture. He brought us out of Egypt. "And he has as it were the strength of the [buffalo] (verse 22, paraphrased). He uses the word "unicorn," but some translations use "buffalo." I'd rather be as strong as the buffalo!

Verses 23-24 tell us, "*Surely there is no enchantment against me or you that can prevail, neither is there any divination against me or you that can prevail. According to this time it shall be said of you and me, Look what the Lord has done!*" (paraphrased) Hallelujah! Glory to God!

He's done something fantastic in Christ. He made a way where there seemed to be no way. He opened a door where there was no door. Jesus opened up heaven to you and me. We can come boldly today to the throne of grace knowing that God loves us, knowing that God is for us.

As a matter of fact, Isaiah 54:17 says no weapon formed against you or me shall prosper. What does that mean? That means no matter what comes at us in life, it cannot and will not succeed if we dare to believe who we are in Christ and who Christ is in us and stand our ground in Jesus' name against the works of the enemy.

He goes on to say in Isaiah 54:17, "*This is the heritage of the children of the Lord, and their righteousness is of me, saith God*" (paraphrased). Hallelujah! Praise God. Nobody can defeat us. No devil can stop us. We win. The curse has been destroyed. Jesus Christ is Lord. God is on our side.

I like what Trina Hankins says: "God is on our side. The blood has been applied. Every need is supplied. Nothing shall be denied. So I enter into rest. I know I am blessed. I have passed the test, and I will get God's best." Many times, what God gave to her are my fightin' words of faith!

The Bible says we are to fight the good fight of faith. When I'm going through the storm, sometimes I just open my mouth and I say this, "God is on my side! The blood has been applied. Every need is supplied. Nothing shall be denied. So I enter into rest. I know I am blessed. I have passed the test, and I will get God's best." Hallelujah! That is a new creation reality. I am blessed. I am redeemed. I am healed. I am loved. I am wanted. I am in the beloved, accepted, and approved of by almighty God. I'm free from the curse of the law—poverty, sickness, and death. I'm righteous, rich, and well. You too are filled with the Godhead—the Father, the Son, and the Holy Ghost. We've got the very life of God in us, the very nature of God in us, and the very love of God in us.

We are free from the religious requirements of this world, those things that try to make us achieve right standing with God on our own. Now I believe in right living and doing right things, but not to be righteous. Our righteousness comes to us as a gift. If I give you a gift, that means you didn't earn it; it's a gift. Enjoy it! Praise the Lord.

Declare you're the righteousness of God in Christ according to 2 Corinthians 5:21. The religious requirements of this old world, the traditions of men that try to put us into bondage, have been broken. We have a first-class freedom in Christ, and we are redeemed. Praise the Lord! Hallelujah!

IN CHRIST, YOU'RE PERFECT

I want to read a couple of verses back in Colossians. I want to remind us of the last two verses of Colossians chapter one where Paul said in 1:28, "*Whom we preach* [he's talking about Jesus], *warning every man, and teaching every man in all wisdom; that we may present every man perfect in Christ Jesus.*" And then he said, "*Whereunto I also labour, striving according to his working, which worketh in me mightily*" (verse 29).

He said, "This is what I'm called to do: to teach on new creation realities. And I want people to know that in Christ, you're perfect." In Christ, you're perfect. Every part is there for spiritual growth and spiritual maturity. There's nothing missing, nothing broken. If you feed on the Word, drink of the Spirit, fellowship with believers, and walk with God, you'll grow into spiritual maturity into the fullness of the statue of the risen Christ. So keep pressing that way! Paul said, "*I press on toward the mark for the prize of the high calling of God* in Christ Jesus" (Philippians 3:14).

And then he goes on in chapter two, "Look, I've had some conflict over this." He said, "The devil don't like what I'm preaching, but I tell you this. You guys encourage me." It's what he said in chapter two. He said in verse two, "You encourage me because I see that your hearts are knit together in love. I see that you are rich in faith, in full assurance of understanding of who you are in Christ." He said, "You got it. You got this message. You embrace this message." And he says, "It blesses me that you're embracing this message of the mystery of God, the mystery of the Father, the mystery of the risen Christ, how that He's working in you and through you and for you."

And then in verse three of Colossians two, He said, "*In whom are hid all the treasures of wisdom and knowledge.*" So since it says, "In whom are hid all the treasures of wisdom and knowledge," that means that all the wisdom I need is in Christ. The wealth I need is in Christ. The blessing I need is in Christ. The knowledge I need is in Christ. I can grow in an understanding of these new creation realities, as I continue in them like this church in Colossians was continuing in the revelation of in Christ realities and new creation realities. Paul said, "I tell you, it blesses me to see you growing in Christ. Because in Him is where all the treasures of God's wisdom and the knowledge of God is hidden."

And then he went on to say this, "*And this I say, lest any man should beguile you with enticing words*" (Colossians 2:4). He said, "You listen. You listen to the Gospel, which is good news in Christ Jesus."

Paul continues, "*For though I be absent in the flesh, yet am I with you in the spirit, joying and beholding your order, and the stedfastness of your faith in Christ*" (Colossians 2:5). These guys were sticking with it. They were saying, "We've got it, and we're going to stick with it. We're going to keep moving in it. We're going to keep affirming it. We're going to keep acknowledging it. We're going to keep living it. We're going to keep showing it. We're going to keep growing in it, because we're called as new creation believers, and we want to understand these new creation realities.

Verse six says, "*As ye have therefore received Christ Jesus the Lord, so walk ye in him.*"

Now that verse really blesses me because it says to us the way we grow is the same way we got saved. The way we continue to know who God is and what God has provided is the same way we got saved. He said that principle works on every level.

What principle was it? He said the way you received Christ Jesus the Lord. How did we receive Him? Well, Romans 10:9-10 says with the heart man believes unto righteousness, and with the mouth confession is made unto salvation. Hallelujah! Praise God. So what does that mean? That means it's a heart and mouth connection. I believe in my heart. I say it with my mouth—Jesus is Lord, and that reality comes into my spirit.

Well, he said that's the same thing you do when you walk in the new creation realities. You believe it. I'm a new creature in Christ, and you speak it. That's who I am. That's what I have. Hallelujah! And just let the reality of that come alive. That's why we use Philemon verse six so much because it says that the communication of your faith may become effectual. Effectual in you, effectual in others, effectual in life by the acknowledging of every good thing that's in you in Christ.

That's also exactly what Romans 10:9-10 says. It's just said in a different way: "*That you believe it in your heart, say it with your mouth.*" Philemon says you acknowledge it with your mouth, the good thing that's in Christ. That's who I am. That's what I have. And it becomes effectual. The reality of it begins to grow in you and emanate from you and affect everything around you. Praise God. Hallelujah. Glory to God. Thank you, Jesus. Amen.

DIG DEEPER

Paul goes on, "*Rooted and built up in him, and stablished in the faith, as ye have been taught, abounding therein with thanksgiving*" (Colossians 2:7). Rooted and built up *in Him*. Wow. You mean I can actually sink my roots *deeper*? Well, yeah. That's what we're doing in this book. We're sinking our roots.

What are the roots? The root is the part of the tree you don't see. It's underground. Well, the root here is your spirit man. Sink the roots of your spirit deep in Christ, deep in new creation realities, so you are built up in Him. If you go deeper, the tree goes higher. If you go deeper, the tree gets wider. If you go deeper, the tree gets stronger. Hallelujah! And what are we doing? We're going deeper in the new creation realities than we've ever been before. How are we doing that? By acknowledging every good thing that's in us in Christ. By noticing those little prepositions in Paul's letters—*in, with, for,* and *through*—and realizing that the power of the Gospel is tied up in those relational prepositions. I am crucified *with* Christ. I'm buried *with* Christ. I'm raised *with* Christ. Now I live *in* Christ because I'm seated *with* Christ, and *through* Him I have been designed to function.

And so with that in mind, we can sink our roots deeper than we've ever gone before. I like the Amplified Bible of that verse a whole lot. It says, "*Have the roots [of your being]* [that's your spirit man] *firmly and deeply planted [in Him fixed and founded in Him], being continually built up in Him, becoming increasingly more confirmed and established in the faith, just as you were taught, and abounding and overflowing in it with thanksgiving.*"

You can abound and overflow in who you are in Christ with a thankful heart. You can sink the roots of your being deeper than ever before. And I love what Paul says, that we are "*fixed and founded.*"

You know, I heard some years ago that the palm tree is a powerful tree. The palm tree gets its life through the center of the tree, not just between the bark and the wood. So that's why they say a palm tree, in hurricane force winds, can take a lickin' and go on tickin' because you've got to cut it down to kill it. And we're really called to be palm tree Christians, just flowing in the breeze. We've got inner life. We don't have surface life. We've got the roots of our being deeply planted in Christ.

There are certain palm trees that are planted in sandy soil. You'd think it would be easy to uproot them with the wind, but the roots of these palm trees go down into the sand and spread out every which way, forming a strong base. So it's got this root base that's spread out, and that's like the strong base of who we are in Christ.

There's another one that just goes down, down, in that sandy soil until it finds a rock down in the sandy soil. It wraps the root around the rock, and so when the winds blow, that thing is wrapped around the rock.

Well, the rock is Christ Jesus, and we're to sink our roots deep! Wrap around the rock and let the wind blow, baby! I ain't goin' *nowhere*! Hallelujah! I've got inner life. I'm wrapped around the rock. I've got the base of who I am in Christ, and everything is gonna be all right!

So sink the roots of our being firmly and deeply in Christ. This is not just a one-time lesson that we read now and never return to. This is a launching pad to launch deeper into the new creation realities. Every day, say something about who Christ is, what Christ did, who you are in Him, and then say, "That's who I am. That's what I have."

DON'T GIVE ME NO BOLOGNA

Paul goes on to say this, "*Beware lest any man spoil you through philosophy and vain deceit, after the tradition of men, after the rudiments of the world, and not after Christ*" (Colossians 2:8). Some people are going to try to get you off of who Christ is and what Christ did. They're going to try and explain it away. They're going to try to get you caught up in the philosophy of life. They'll say things like, "Why does God heal some and God doesn't heal some? God does this and God does that. Sometimes God's happy. Sometimes God's mad at you." Where do you find that? You can't find it in the New Covenant. Not since Jesus died and rose from the dead.

Here's one example. Doctors are great. I'm not saying we shouldn't go to doctors. But I'm just saying don't go to one that really nullifies the work of Christ, doesn't believe in God, doesn't think that the Bible is true. You can find a lot of good doctors that are also good Christians and have faith in God. But don't go to someone that tries to undermine who Christ is and talk you out of the blessing or talk you out of your healing.

So Paul says, beware of that. I love the Cotton Patch version. For Colossians 2:8, he says this: "Watch your step, now. And don't let anybody make a sucker out of you with his intellectual jazz and his smooth sounding bologna." Don't give me no bologna! Give me life in Christ.

He said, "This bologna is based on human concoctions and on worldly standards and not on Christ." We are to focus our attention on Jesus. Verses nine and ten say, "*For in him dwelleth all the fulness of the Godhead bodily. And ye* [and I] *are complete in him, which is the head of all principality and power*" (brackets TM).

Redeemed by the blood of the Lamb, we stand in Christ today. We're sinking our roots deeper than we've ever gone, before because we too are in Him, and we are filled with the Godhead. No bologna for us—just a deeper and deeper relationship with God through His new creation realities.

CHAPTER 9:

BROUGHT NEAR THROUGH CHRIST

In the previous chapter, we talked about our redemption in Christ and digging deeply so we are firmly rooted on the Rock that is Christ Jesus our Lord. We're going to talk about how we are *brought near* through Christ.

I want us to get this image: you are not an outsider. You've been brought near. We are not outside of the covenant. We know that, but more than that, *we're seated right next to God.* In His mind and in His plan, we can snuggle up next to Him knowing He's our Father. He's our Abba Father, our Daddy God.

We are going to look at this truth starting in Ephesians 2:8, which says, "*For by grace are ye saved through faith; and that not of yourselves: it is the gift of God.*"

So what is the gift of God? Well, salvation is a gift of God, and so is faith, and certainly so is grace. It's all the gift of God. But I want to point out that verse for this reason. Some folks say, "We're saved by grace," and they focus just on grace. We should focus on grace; without grace we don't have any salvation.

But notice it says, "*By grace are ye saved through faith.*" So grace and faith go together. We access the grace of God by faith in God. There are a lot of people who have already been saved in the mind of God because He already provided Jesus as a free gift of grace, but they haven't accepted it by faith, so it really doesn't do them any good.

If I put something on deposit for you at the bank, it's there. It's yours in your name, but you've got to go receive it. So let's never forget that **faith and grace work together**. We are called to live by faith in God's grace, through Christ. Through faith we inherit the promises of God. That's who we are—men and women of faith because of God's great grace.

Paul said, "*not of works, lest any man should boast*" (Ephesians 2:9). That means our salvation isn't something we did on our own. It's something He gave to us. It's a gift not of works, lest you could brag, "Well, I did this. And I did this. And I did this. And you didn't do that, so God loves me more." No, no, no. God loves us all the same. And righteousness is a gift that comes to us through faith in Christ Jesus. We have been made the righteousness of God in Christ.

Remember, righteousness is a noun. It has to do with what was imparted to you in the new birth. I say the gene of God's righteousness was imparted to me. That makes me stand up tall and sit up straight. I've got His nature, His life, His love, and His righteousness in me.

GET READY TO LIVE THE GOOD LIFE

Paul writes, "*For we are his workmanship, created in Christ Jesus unto good works, which God hath before ordained that we should walk in them*" (Ephesians 2:10). Now that's amazing.

God's got an ordained path and an ordained plan for you and me. And I can walk in it by faith in Christ. Praise God! We're not reading this book by accident. I don't believe we're here at this space in time by accident. God called us to the kingdom for such a time as this! And we can be assured that we are recreated in Christ unto good works, which He has ordained that we should walk in them. The Amplified Bible says, "*taking paths which he prepared ahead of time, that we should walk in them*" (verse 10). And then it says, "*Living the good life which He prearranged and made ready for us to live*" (verse 10, AMPC).

That's a good confession, isn't it? I'm living the good life in Christ that God prearranged and made ready for me to live. I'm going to walk right into my good life. I'm going to walk right into God's plan. By faith, I say that's who I am; that's what I have. And God brings that reality into my life. Praise the Lord! Hallelujah! Thank you, Jesus. Amen.

So I wanted to remind us of those particular Scriptures there—that it's by grace through faith and that we are His handiwork. He's got plans for us, predestined for us, and as we acknowledge that, we begin to walk that out and walk into that God-prepared place.

Now, verse 11, "*Wherefore remember, that ye being in time past Gentiles in the flesh, who are called Uncircumcision by that which is called the Circumcision in the flesh made by hands.*" So he's saying, "Look, there was a time when you were not a covenant person. You had no covenant with God."

Verse 12 says, "*That at that time ye were without Christ, being aliens from the commonwealth of Israel, and strangers from the covenants of promise, having no hope, and without God in the world.*" Now he's talking to us about what we were, so we can really understand and appreciate who we are. It's not too often in the Bible that God tells us to remember what we were. But this verse does for a simple reason: Paul is pointing out the magnitude of our redemption—how great it really is and how it encompasses all that God has for us. We are not a second choice. We are not just warmed-over stew. We don't get the leftovers. We get the real deal in Christ! The fullness of God, the fullness of the God-head, the fullness of God's plan, is ours today in Christ.

I remember those days when I was not walking with Christ. And I'm so glad that I'm walking with Christ today. We were "*strangers from the covenants of promise, having no hope, and* [we were] *without God in the world*" (verse 12, brackets TM). This was a bleak picture! Verses 11-12 paint for us the picture of our life without Christ—that we were strangers from the covenants of God. We had no hope in the world. We were without God.

But thank God for verse 13! God's about to say something different! It says, "*But now in Christ Jesus ye who sometimes were far off are made nigh by the blood of Christ.*" That's one of my favorite *in Christ* Scriptures.

The Amplified says you are "*brought near*" by the blood of Jesus Christ. Hallelujah! We are brought near by the blood of Jesus Christ. We are redeemed by the blood of Jesus Christ. We were over here, and we had no hope. We were outside the covenant, but now we are made nigh, brought near, by the blood of Jesus. So we could say now, "I'm not far off. I'm not far out (outside the covenant, that is). I'm not away from God. God lives in me. God lives in you. Praise God, He's very near, and I'm very near to Him."

Paul said, "Now I am in covenant with God. Now I do have Christ. Now I am not a stranger and a foreigner to the promises of God. Now I am blessed in Christ. Now I am not a stranger anymore. Now I have hope. I have God in my life." Christ within us is the hope of glory, and He's got some wonderful plans for me and for you. Hallelujah! Thank God for the love of God, and the grace of God, and who we are in Christ. Now in Christ we are brought near.

WE ALWAYS HAVE HOPE

Do you remember Jeremiah 29:11? You probably know this verse. It says, "*For I know the thoughts that I think toward you, saith the Lord, thoughts of peace, and not of evil, to give you hope in your final outcome*" (KJV and AMPC paraphrase). Or: to give you expectation in the end. In other words, God said we are never in life without hope anymore. For us under the New Covenant, Jesus is our hope. Jesus is our strength. And the Amplified Bible says, "*I have thoughts and plans of peace, not of evil, to give you hope in your final outcome*" (Jeremiah 29:11, paraphrased).

So you may be going through a struggle right now, but don't forget—in Christ, you're brought near. And don't forget that God has a plan and a purpose for your life. He's got hope in your final outcome. So just keep walking out the plan of God. Keep worshipping God. Keep loving God and loving people. And you know what? He'll work it out. God's got more than one way to figure out how to get you out of your trouble and how to bring you into your place—your wealthy place, your large place, your blessing place. God will bring His Word to pass. Don't give up. Don't give in. Speak up. Look up. Stand up. And decree, "If God be for me, who's going to be against me?" Play till you win. The devil can't stop you. God is for you. We win! Hallelujah! Glory to God.

Look at 2 Corinthians 2:14: "*Now thanks be unto God, which always causeth us to triumph in Christ.*" Did you see that? It said "always," as in every place.

Think back to those verses the Apostle Paul wrote in Ephesians two about who we were before; he wanted to remind us of who we were so we could really enjoy who we are. Hallelujah! He said you *were*, but now you *are*. Because of Christ, we have been brought near. Because of Christ, God is with us. Because of Christ, we are never without the Lord.

Sometimes you can feel alone. Sometimes you may look alone. But I'm telling you, *you are not alone*. The Holy One of Israel is with you. The Greater One, the Holy Spirit, lives on the inside of you, and your help comes from the Lord who made heaven and earth (Psalm 121:2). It's pretty good when you've got God helping you. He's an expert. The Holy Spirit is a genius. And He's on our side. The blood's been applied. And every need shall be supplied.

Go back to verse 13, "*But now in Christ Jesus ye who sometimes were far off are made nigh by the blood of Christ.*" You were, but now you are. Hallelujah! Praise God. So I see myself snuggled right up next to the Father. I see myself sitting with Jesus in heavenly places. And I sing this song:

I have been redeemed through the blood of Jesus Christ.
I have been redeemed by the supreme sacrifice.
I have been brought near to the heart of the living God.
I've been reconciled.

I love 2 Corinthians 5:19 in the Cotton Patch version. It says, "*It was God in Christ, hugging the world to Himself.*" I like to see myself hugged by Jesus every day. God's hugging me right now. Hallelujah! God's hugging you too. See yourself brought near in Christ. See yourself welcomed into the throne room. Visualize yourself sitting right there at the right hand of God in Christ. The

Bible says we're raised up with Him to sit with Him in heavenly places. See yourself with total access today.

Come boldly to the throne of grace. Boldly means confidently—not arrogantly, but confidently—knowing that you're loved, knowing that you're wanted. Come boldly to the throne of grace. Walk right into the throne room just like Jesus. You're in Jesus. You're redeemed by Jesus. **God loves you as much He does Jesus!** Because of the blood of Jesus Christ, we can come into the very presence without a sense of guilt or shame or fear because we know God hugged us and is hugging us unto Himself, and drawing us near today.

We can come with assurance that we're wanted and that we're loved by God. We know we are redeemed. We are bought back by God because He wanted us, He needed us, and He loved us. The Bible said He "*dearly prized*" us (AMPC). He couldn't live without you. He said, "No, no, no. I'm not willing to do that. I'm going to give my very best for them. I'm not willing to live without them." And He sent Jesus to bring us into the family of God. Hallelujah! Praise the Lord. Thank you, Jesus.

Look at Ephesians 2:14-15, "*For he* [talking about Jesus] *is our peace, who hath made both one, and hath broken down the middle wall of partition between us; Having abolished* [done away with] *in his flesh the enmity, even the law of commandments contained in ordinances; for to make in himself of twain one new man, so making peace.*"

Jesus came as a propitiation, the bridge, the gap-filler, the one who restores favor, and He made of the two—Gentile and Jew—one new person—a Jesus man, a Jesus woman, a new creature in Christ Jesus. You and I are born of God. We are filled with His Spirit. We are called by His name. And we have come together in Christ for such a time as this!

I have a song that says:

"Jesus came to make one out of the two.
In His body reconciled, Gentile and Jew.
Hanging there on the cross the work was done.
I have been grafted in as a son.
I have been grafted into the vine.
I am His, thank God, and He is mine.
I have left the old nature far behind me.
I have been grafted into the vine."

We've been grafted into the vine. We're one with Him. One new man out of the two. We are in Christ. We're no longer without God. We are reconnected to God. Jesus made it possible, and in Him we live, and move, and have our being. We are now the covenant people of God! Hallelujah! Praise God!

Look at verse 16, "*And that he might reconcile both unto God in one body by the cross, having slain the enmity thereby.*"

Now you know the word "enmity" means a hostility or hatred. We're seeing some of that today. Who would ever think that would happen again and again in America. Animosity, strong dislike, strong disapproval displayed in actions—that's enmity. So I bind that spirit of enmity in our nation, in the land. We proclaim *freedom* in Christ Jesus, *peace* in Christ Jesus! And we can live in peace that passes all understanding because He has reconciled both Jew and Gentile. Now that means everybody. In God's mind, the classifications were Jew or Gentile. Gentile would include everybody that wasn't born a Jew.

Verse 17 goes on, "*And came and preached peace to you which were afar off, and to them that were nigh.*" Now at that time, he was talking about the Jewish nation, which is the one who had the covenant, and Christ came to preach peace to *all of us* and make one new man out of the two. We have been, grafted in as a son or a daughter of God. Hallelujah!

Verse 18, "*For through him we both have access by one Spirit unto the Father.*" Did you see that? Look at that little verse and look at what it says again. "For through him...." There's that word *through*—through Him.

Can you imagine a little verse including so much? Can you see Jesus in that verse? Can you see in that verse Gentile and Jew? Can you see in that verse the Holy Spirit? Can you see in that verse the Father? All of them are in there in one little verse. Through Jesus we both—that's Gentile and Jew—have access by one Spirit, the Holy Spirit, unto the Father. So you've got the Father, and the Son, and the Holy Ghost, and you, and me in one verse!

One translation says, "*We have an introduction by one Spirit to the Father because of Jesus.*" In other words, you're introduced to God as your Father and you as His child by the Holy Spirit in Christ Jesus. We are all sons and daughters of God in Christ Jesus. So that little verse contains the whole picture of redemption.

We are found in Him. And because of Him we have this introduction to God through the function—through the purpose—we live our life through what Christ did. He's our High Priest. He represents us today. He's opened up heaven for us today.

I like to say we have total access. I like to say we have security clearance. I can just say this, that *in Christ* we can always run to God. We don't have to run from God; we run *to* God. Hallelujah! And He is the One who loves us. He's the One who planned the plan of redemption for us. He's our very own Father.

LIVE IN THE NOW

I love the word "now," particularly the word "now" in the New Testament. In many cases in Paul's writing, the word "now" represents a new creation reality. The word "now" does that because in many cases—not in every, but in many cases—it differentiates between what was and what is because of Christ. "Now" can become a new creation term. And so I've circled a lot of those in my Bible because I found that out years ago that it *was*, but *now* it's changed. It's like you *were* without God, but *now* in Christ, you have access.

There's another "now" in Ephesians 2:19 I want you to see: "*Now therefore ye are no more strangers and foreigners, but fellowcitizens with the saints, and of the household of God.*" So this verse says it again. It repeats what was said in verse 11-12. You were in the world without God. You had no hope. It refutes that by saying this: "*Now therefore ye are no more strangers....*" Remember that word earlier was an alien and a stranger from covenant. You are no longer strangers. Now you are no longer foreigners, but you are a fellow citizen with the saints, and you belong to the household of God!

So it's saying exactly what verse 13 said, only it amplifies it and reminds us that we are not strangers. We are not foreigners. We are not in the world without God. We are not a people who do not have hope. We are fellow citizens with the saints, and we belong to the household of God. So we are fellow citizens, and we are family members. Praise God! So we've got some rights and some privileges as citizens, and we've got some rights and privileges as sons and daughters. Praise God!

That's who I am. Is that who you are today? That's who I am in Christ. In Christ I'm a fellow citizen. In Christ I'm a household member. In Christ I'm not a stranger to the covenant. Now I don't know all I'm going to know, but what I know I'm going to stick with—Christ in me the hope of glory. Christ is for me, not against me. Christ loves me; He's on my side. Christ is helping me, and lifting me, and showing me, and teaching me. He's not pushing me down, pushing me back, and making me sick. No, I'm the righteousness of God in Christ! Hallelujah! I've got right standing. I've got access. I've got an introduction to the Father. God knows me. Hallelujah! He knows you too. We know Him, and we're getting to know Him better.

So, now therefore you're no more a stranger. You're no more a foreigner. You're no more an outsider. Praise God you've got friends in high places. And you're a fellow citizen with the saints, and you belong to the household of God. Hallelujah! Praise God.

TAKE OUR DOMINION

Now let's go on. He says, "*And are built upon the foundation of the apostles and prophets, Jesus Christ himself is holding this thing together*" (verse 20, paraphrased). Jesus Christ Himself is the chief cornerstone. He's holding this thing together. It's built in Him. He's the chief. He's the Lord. He's the head, and we're the body. We're in Him. We're connected. Hallelujah! You think the Church, the body of Christ, is not important? Let me tell you, the Church of the living God, the believers today on this planet, is the most important group on the planet.

God has given us authority. God has given us dominion, and we're to use that dominion against the strategies and the wiles of the devil. If we stand back and don't proclaim righteousness, peace, and joy in the Holy Ghost—if we stand back and don't use the name of Jesus against the enmity and the strife and the demonic activity in the earth today—the devil will surely prevail because there is no other group on the planet that has the authority to stop the enemy but the Church of the living God.

I like to say we've been deputized by the Giver of Life. We're sent forth to conquer outlaw spirits and set the captives free. We've been authorized in the mighty name of Jesus, so we take our sword, the Word of God, and we arrest the enemy. Somebody's got to tell the devil to stop! Somebody's got to tell him to shut up! Somebody's got to tell him to back off! And that somebody is the Church of the living God!

You are the righteousness of God in Christ for a reason. It's not just for personal blessing, although it includes that. But it is for dominion. It's for the power of Christ to be exerted through us and in us for righteousness' sake in the earth today. Somebody's got to stand against the enemy. Somebody has to stand up for those that cannot stand up for themselves. Somebody has to say, "No!" to the devil, and "yes" to God. Somebody has to hold the hand of faith and say, "Stop! In Jesus' name!" And stand against the works of darkness, praying for our nation, lifting up our voice, using the authority that's given to us as sons and daughters of the living God.

In Christ we rule and reign. We are kings and priests of God! Let's take our dominion! It has been restored to us. That's not just an opinion. That is the truth of the Word of God. Jesus said, "*I will give unto you the keys of the kingdom of heaven, and whatsoever you bind on earth will be bound in heaven; whatsoever you loose on earth will be loosed in heaven*!" (Matthew 16:19) We are in Christ for this season! Rise up! Take the name that's above every name and run the devil out of town! Hallelujah! Run him out of your life! Stand fast and strong against the works of darkness.

This is what the Lord said to me. I'll give it to you: "So be the light. Get it right. Walk in His power, love, and might. We have a place by His grace. So put a smile on your face. Stop the enemy. Set the captive free, because we have been given the authority." Hallelujah! We are built up in Christ for such a time as this.

WE NEED EACH OTHER

"*In whom all the building fitly framed together groweth unto an holy temple in the Lord*" (Ephesians 2:21). We need each other. We need God working in us individually but also collectively. Find a good church to get involved with. Thank God you're learning who you are in Christ, but I tell you, find a good church. Be a part of the family of God. Work together to build the kingdom of God. Stand your ground against the devil. Don't give him an inch. Rebuke him, resist him, and he will flee from you the Bible said in James. That means he will run from you in terror as when someone's hair stands on end. The devil is really concerned about you and me getting this message of who we are in Christ, because He knows once we get it, we'll rise up in faith, love, and power and demonstration of the Holy Ghost, and we're going to take over some stuff. Hallelujah! We'll stop the works of darkness and promote the works of Christ. The Bible tells us to put on the armor of light (Romans 13:12) and go forward in faith and fight the good fight.

So these verses are important to us because they tell us that Jesus is the one holding this together. He gave us His name. He gave us His authority. And then verse 21 said, "*In whom all the building fitly framed together groweth....*" So we're growing when we're fitly framed together. You're really not designed to be just an isolated individual on your own. Even though salvation is a personal thing, it's also a community thing—it's the community of Christ, working together, loving each other, praying with one another, lifting up the Name of Jesus. And then he said you will grow unto a holy temple in the Lord (Ephesians 2:21). There's one verse that says that when every part of the body is working together it causes increase in the fullness of God and increase that comes from God. Praise the Lord! Hallelujah! So we need each other.

And then finally in that chapter it says, "*In whom ye also are builded together for an habitation of God through the Spirit*" (verse 22). So God's interested in us being a habitation of God, a place where the Spirit of God hangs out. We're to be a place where the life of God is evident, a place where the gifts of the Spirit flow. Gifts of healing. Working of miracles. Signs and wonders. Praise the Lord! Hallelujah! We're to be a place where joy flows and people get happy because they're in love with Jesus and because of Who He is and what He's done.

Paul said, "*You are built together for a habitation of God through the Spirit.*" So it's not just a visitation that we need, although, a visitation is wonderful. It's not just an outpouring because an outpouring seems like it ends. But how about this—a *habitation* where we walk and live in the presence and power of God.

Now, I believe in an outpouring. May the Lord send one! But I want to live in the power of His love. I want to live in the light of these new creation realities. I want to live loving people, lifting Jesus, and letting the Holy Spirit have His way. That's habitation!

GO TO THE UPPER ROOM

Don't put the Holy Spirit back in the corner somewhere. I pastored a church for thirty-two years. The Lord told me, "I want you to give the Holy Spirit a reserved seat on the front row." So I said, "OK! Right there! You've got reserved seating, a reserved position in this community."

So I'm just saying we want a habitation of the Holy Spirit in our life personally—a reserved seat just for Him—in our churches and in our fellowship with God.

I like to say this: There's a virgin womb. There's an empty tomb. But there's power for believers in the upper room. And I believe that "upper room" experience is just as much of a new creation reality as your salvation. Jesus died on the cross, not just to forgive our sins, but to set us free from Satan's dominion. He raised us from the dead so we could have a new life. And then He sent His Spirit to fill us with overflowing presence and power with the Person of the Holy Spirit. Have you been filled with the Holy Spirit since you believed?

Let me encourage you as a Christian. Go on into the upper room. Don't stop at the empty tomb. Thank God for the empty tomb; we've got to have that. I mean, if Jesus is dead, we're in trouble. But go on to the upper room. Experience the outpouring of the Holy Spirit for your life personally like they did on the day of Pentecost when there was a rushing mighty wind that came into the place, and they were all filled with the Holy Spirit and began to speak with other tongues as the Spirit gave them utterance.

Speaking in other tongues simply means a language of the Spirit flowing out of your spirit, through your mouth, enabling you to pray in line with the perfect will of God. It enables you to edify yourself and build yourself up on your most holy faith, praying in the Holy Ghost.

So the Bible says here that the ultimate goal that God had in Christ was to make us a habitation of the Spirit of God. It wasn't just to set us free; although, He did set us free. But it was to make us a habitation of the Spirit of God.

I like to say, "Holy Spirit, you are welcome in my life today." I like to welcome Him into my life and recognize Him every day because He's the One who helps us and teaches us the Word of God, and we are built together by Christ for a habitation of God through the Spirit.

WHAT JESUS HAD TO SAY ABOUT THE HOLY SPIRIT

Now let's just take one look at the role of the Holy Spirit. What is He going to do when He comes? Well, if we're built together for a habitation of God, then we might want to look at what Jesus said about Him because Jesus had a lot to say about the Holy Spirit. Let's look at a couple of verses. In John 16:6 Jesus said this: "*But because I have said these things unto you, sorrow hath filled your heart.*" Jesus was talking to His disciples. He had just told them that He was going away, and He was going to send the Holy Spirit. They said, "We don't want you to go!" He said, "Let me tell you something." Verse 7: "*Nevertheless I tell you the truth; It is expedient for you that I go away.*"

"Expedient" means "advantageous." He's saying, "It's to your advantage that I go away." You see, when Jesus was on the earth, He was limited to one place at one time. But now through His death, burial, resurrection, ascension, and sending the Holy Spirit, He is everywhere all the time. He can be in you. He can be in me. He can be in Albuquerque. He can be in Tulsa. He can be in India. He's everywhere. Glory to God. Hallelujah! Thank you, Jesus. Amen.

So it's advantageous, Jesus said, that I go away. For if I go not away, the Holy Spirit will not come. But if I go, I will send Him unto you (John 16:7 paraphrased). And then He said, "*And when he comes, he will convince the world of sin, of righteousness, and of judgment*" (verse 8). He will convince them of sin, because they believe not on me (verse 9 paraphrased). So he said that's the main thing that people need to do is to come to faith in Christ. He will convince the world of righteousness, because I go to my Father, and you see me no more (verse 10 paraphrased).

Basically, He was saying, "You know, you're not going to see Me anymore, but they're going to see you. They're going to see Me in you." They're going to see that we are in Christ, filled with the Spirit of God, and they're going to recognize that this Jesus is *real.* I can tell you right now, if you'd have known me before I was saved, and you know me now that I've gotten saved, you'd say, "That had to be God! God must be real." And I could probably say the same thing about you. And people that knew you then and that know you now, they can see Christ in you. That's the righteousness of God. That's the nature of God being displayed in us because we are in Christ. Hallelujah! And the Holy Spirit is there to amplify that, to help us with that.

And then He said He's going to convince the world of judgment, because the prince of this world is judged (John 16:11 paraphrased). Hallelujah!

I have a song that I used to sing,

"Judged, judged, judged, judged,
the devil and all his works are judged.
Judged, judged, judged, judged, judged,
the devil and all his works are judged.
Since the Holy Spirit came and gave to us a new name,
the devil is judged."

That means he's defeated. If he's judged, that means sentence has already been passed upon him. Hallelujah! We are in the victory parade of Christ, and the enemy is defeated, and he's under our feet.

So Jesus says the Holy Spirit convinces us of that. He convinces us that we are living in Christ. He convinces us that we really are who God says we are and we can do what God says we can do and we have what God says we have. Praise God for the help of the Holy Spirit! He convinces us Jesus Christ is Lord. So we work with the Holy Spirit. We welcome the Holy Spirit. Jesus introduced the Holy Spirit to the Church. That was His ultimate plan in redemption—to forgive us, to raise us from the dead, to seat us in heavenly places, and to fill us with the Holy Ghost. Hallelujah!

And then Jesus said, "*I've got many things to tell you, but you can't bear them now*" (John 16:12 paraphrased) What things? Well, some are things that we've been studying in this book!

Jesus hadn't gone to the cross yet when He was talking to them in John 16. He said, "I've got many things to share with you about what's gonna happen. It's gonna be better than you think. It's gonna be awesome. I'm going to go to the cross. I'm going to rise from the dead. I'm going to send the Holy Spirit. He's going to fill you, and thrill you, and cause you to live life victoriously in me." He said, "I can't tell you all of that yet...." But now watch: "*When the Holy Spirit comes, He will guide you into all truth....*" (verse 13a)

The Holy Spirit has been guiding us in our *in Christ* realities, in our new creation realities. He will guide us who are in Christ into all truth—what God did for us in Christ. "*He shall not speak of himself; but whatever he hears from heaven, he will speak to you, and he will show you things to come*" (verse 13). Hallelujah!

So the Holy Spirit is transmitting to us heaven's will, heaven's plan, and God's mind. He is teaching us the Word of God. He is helping us walk in an overcoming life. He is filling us with revelation knowledge of who we are in Christ. We have been brought near to the heart of God, and we are built together so the Holy Spirit can come inhabit us and fill us and help us and strengthen us.

You could say this: That the Holy Spirit's job is to draw us near to Christ. Let the Holy Spirit work in you today. Welcome Him into your life, and let Jesus Christ be Lord. If you want to grasp who you are in Christ so that it becomes your lifestyle, you need a Teacher. And thankfully, Jesus left us the best one in the universe, His very Spirit.

CHAPTER 10:

ZERO CONDEMNATION

In the previous chapter, we looked at how we are drawn near to Christ. It is an amazing process, and at the end of the chapter I showed you the role the Holy Spirit plays in drawing us near and teaching us everything we need for a life of godliness.

I want to start this next chapter in the eighth chapter of Romans. This is one of my favorite chapters in the whole Bible. And we're going to have a great time talking about this new creation reality—that there is *Zero Condemnation in Christ.*

So Romans 8:1 says, "*There is therefore now no condemnation to them which are in Christ Jesus.*" If you stepped out of Adam into Christ through the new birth, by accepting Jesus as Lord and being born of the Spirit, then you're in Christ and "*there is therefore now no* [**ZERO**] *condemnation to them which are in Christ Jesus, who walk not after the flesh, but after the Spirit*" (Romans 8:1 brackets TM).

That phrase means you're not depending on the works of the flesh for your righteousness. You're depending on the work in the Spirit that Christ did for us, and through the help of the Holy

Spirit, you're walking in the righteousness that He made you to be. Remember, righteousness is not just behavior. Righteousness will produce good behavior, but righteousness is a noun, and it really means the very gene of righteousness that's in God, Who fathered us in Christ, is part of us.

So, *condemn* means this: "to judge adversely." It would also mean a strong disapproval. Condemnation is any act that condemns. Or, it could be in many cases—this is the case with people—condemnation can be a state of being condemned. People just live with guilty feelings—guilty about their past, guilty about what they said, guilty about what they did—and **Jesus sets us free from that state of being condemned or guilty.** Praise God. Hallelujah! Thank you, Jesus. Amen.

Sometimes I think people in general think God's mad at them. They think some days He gets up on the good side of the bed, and other days He gets up on the bad side of the bed. Well, the good news is He never sleeps. So, He never gets up on either side of the bed! He's always the same.

I heard a story about one lady who met another lady early in the morning, and she asked her, "Did you wake up grumpy this morning?"

She said, "No, I let him sleep."

So some people wake up grumpy. But God doesn't wake up grumpy. He's eternally good. God is good. God is love. God is merciful. But, people have been taught all kinds of stuff when it comes to who God is and how God acts. They credit Him with acts of violence and acts of destruction. They call it an "act of God." Well, that's the devil just trying to paint a bad picture of who God really is. God is not "strongly disapproving" of you.

God told me one time, "I'm not mad at you. And I'll never be mad at you." And I found a Scripture in Isaiah 54 that says that.

He said, "Just like I promise I'd never flood the earth, put the rainbow up in the sky to remind you and me that I'll never re-flood the earth, I promise you that I'll never be mad at you again. I release my anger on Jesus for your sake. For your sake as your substitute and now my loving kindness will never depart from thee" (Isaiah 54:9-10 paraphrased).

You say, "Well, what about when I miss it and mess up?" Well, then you miss it. You made a mistake. We ask God to forgive us. But we don't jump back into a different *condition.* **Your condition is righteousness forever in Christ.** When you make a mistake, just get out of the mistake. Don't get caught in the stumble. Get up and go forward.

Another meaning for condemnation is to pronounce guilty. Well, on the contrary, God in Christ pronounced you and me innocent. He pronounced us free. The Bible plainly says that God openly declared that those who believe in Jesus are righteous—are free from all guilt, sin, *and* condemnation.

And then the last meaning for the word "condemned" would be "to sentence to punishment." Now, God is not going to sentence you to punishment. Somebody says, "Well, I've got to pay for my sins." Why? Jesus paid for them. Now, I understand in the natural that if you break the law, there is a consequence, but I'm talking about spiritually. Being constantly condemned, feeling like God's punishing you, feeling like you never get a break, always talking about the negative side—those are not for us. There is now no condemnation—zero—for those who are in Christ Jesus. Come on, start talking about the positive side of who you are in Christ. You are in Christ and you're free from all judgment, all disapproval, all guilt, and all punishment. Hallelujah! Thank you, Jesus. Amen.

ISAIAH 53

We'll come right back to Romans, but this is a prophetic word that you and I need to know and remember where it is. Let's read the first five verses of Isaiah 53. It says, "*Who hath believed our report? and to whom is the arm of the Lord revealed?*" Now, understand this whole chapter is a prophesy about the coming of Christ. "*For he shall grow up before him as a tender plant, and as a root out of a dry ground: he hath no form nor comeliness; and when we shall see him, there is no beauty that we should desire him. He is despised and rejected of men; a man of sorrows, and acquainted with grief: and we hid as it were our faces from him; he was despised, and we esteemed him not. Surely he hath borne our griefs, and carried our sorrows: yet we did esteem him stricken, smitten of God, and afflicted. But he was wounded* **for** [there's that little word] *our transgressions, he was bruised for our iniquities: the chastisement of our peace was upon him; and with his stripes we are healed*" (Isaiah 53:1, 2-5, brackets TM).

That whole chapter talks about the coming Messiah, what He'd do, who He'd be, and how it would affect you and me. And these verses say right here that He was wounded for us. He was bruised for us. The chastisement of our peace—or shalom, or well-being, prosperity included—was upon Him, and by His stripes we are healed. Praise God. Healing is ours today in Christ! Blessing is ours today in Christ! Forgiveness is ours today in Christ! Thank God we are the righteousness of God in Christ.

And then it said, "*Surely he hath borne our griefs, and carried our sorrows*" (Isaiah 53:4). Did you know that the word "borne" in that scripture is the Hebrew word "*nasa*?" *Nasa* means to carry away. It means to be taken off of, to take off, to be carried away, or to lift off. So in other words, surely He *lifted off* of us our griefs and our sorrows, our pains, and our sickness. That must be believed and received.

Some people think, "Well, God just made me sick to teach me a lesson." No, He did not do that—no more than you would make your child sick to teach them a lesson. You would instruct them. You would show them. They may slip up and get symptoms or sickness in their body, but it's not because *you* put it on them. And that's the same way with our Father God.

He took all this from us—sickness, iniquity, and condemnation. We're no longer condemned. There is *zero* condemnation that has any right in our life. He took our sin, and He took our shame. He took our judgment. He paid the price and the penalty. Now we are free and forgiven and in Christ Jesus.

If you make a mistake, like I say, get up and get going. Move toward God. Get on with life. Hallelujah! Don't get caught in yesterday's mistake or last hour's mistake. Get on with life. Get on with your forgiveness. If you need to ask God to forgive you, do it. If you need to ask someone else to forgive you, do it. We don't live our lives hurting people and making mistakes on purpose. We are new creatures in Christ. We have a love nature. We have a God nature. We have a good nature, and *no* condemnation. Begin to declare Romans 8:1: "*There is therefore now no condemnation in me today because I'm in Christ Jesus.*" Hallelujah!

FREE FROM THE LAW OF SIN AND DEATH

Back in Romans 8:2 it says, "*For the law of the Spirit of life in Christ Jesus hath made me free from the law of sin and death.*" Hallelujah! We're under the New Covenant. It's a love covenant. We're commanded to love God and love one another and love people. We're not under the law of sin and death, the Old

Covenant that pointed out all of our failures and shortcomings. No human could keep the law. As a matter of fact, the Bible said the law's purpose was to show us that we couldn't do it. But Jesus came and fulfilled the law, and He gave to us a new commandment that we love one another. He changed our condition. Hallelujah! We're not just trying to be good. We've been made the righteousness of God.

We're not *trying* to be right. We've *already* been made right with God.

That's who I am, right there. That's what I have. The law of the spirit of life in Christ has made me free from the law of sin and death (Romans 8:2). A law will work if you put it to work. You and I are to speak it and decree it and acknowledge it according to Philemon 1:6.

We believe and speak and act like the Bible's true. That's a simple definition of faith. Believe and speak and act like the Bible's true. Praise God. Hallelujah! And the truth that we know will set us free. The Old Covenant depended upon our ability to keep it. The New Covenant is based on Christ and His ability to keep it *for us*—His grace, and His goodness, and His provision for us. He did it for me, so I could die with Him, be raised with Him, and be seated with Him.

Now I am *in* Him. You remember the word *in*, don't you? "In" means union. I'm united with Him. And through Him, by His help, and by His grace, and by His Word, I function in life. Faith in Him sets us free, for the law of the Spirit of life in Christ has made me free from the law of sin and death.

Look at verse three: "*For what the law could not do, in that it was weak through the flesh....*" The law couldn't do this. It took God sending His own Son in the likeness of sinful flesh and for sin, condemning sin in the flesh. What does it mean that He condemned it? He judged it. **He judged you in Christ as worthy of righteousness.** Praise God!

"*That the righteousness of the law might be fulfilled in us, who walk not after the flesh, but after the Spirit*" (Romans 8:4). Simply said, we are pursuing the things of the Spirit of God in Christ. We're going after Him. We're going after what Jesus did. We're not trying to make our own way. We're not trying to make our own righteousness. We're not trying to wear those filthy rags of self-righteousness.

We have put on the righteousness of Christ. Thank God what the law could not do, God did. We're to follow after the New Covenant, not after the Old Covenant. Praise God, you can learn from the old, types and shadows of the coming Messiah, but don't live there. Live in the new. We're a new creation. We're learning about living in Christ, the life we were meant to live. Live in the New Testament.

Spend time meditating on *in Him, in whom, in Christ.* Spend your time meditating on the love of God. Spend your time learning how faith works and what grace really is and what Jesus has done, and how the Holy Spirit is working in you today. You and I are somebody in Christ, going somewhere to do something awesome for Jesus! Hallelujah!

E.W. Kenyon said that the Law of sin and death—basically, the Old Covenant—was never given for new creation people. We've been given a new creation law, which is the royal law of love. It's a law of the Spirit of life in Christ. It's the law of faith in the blood of Jesus and the Word of God, and we're to live in new creation realities.

Remember that Jesus inaugurated a new agreement or a New Testament or a new way of living, sealed by His own blood. The word *inaugurate* means a formal beginning of something. When Jesus rose from the dead, took His blood to the heavenly Holy of Holies, sent the Holy Spirit—I want you to know that was a formal beginning of something new. Inaugurate also means "to initiate." The word "initiate" means to begin something or set something moving. So, Jesus set something moving in God's direction—moving in the direction of *zoe*, moving in the direction of forgiveness and peace and joy in the Holy Ghost.

It can also mean to originate something. There never was a New Covenant before. God's blood had not been shed before. Now His blood, the blood of God's Son, *God's blood,* was shed for you and me. We didn't need any more lambs. God sent His Lamb. Hallelujah! He's the Lamb that takes away the sins of the world.

Under the Old Covenant they brought their lambs and sacrificed to God. Under the New Covenant, God sent His Lamb for us, on our behalf—one time for all of us, forever the blood of Christ was shed. So walk in the light of the New Covenant. Walk in the light of living in Christ.

CRUCIFIED WITH CHRIST

Let's take another detour. We'll come back to Romans 8, but Galatians 2:20 says this: "***I am** crucified with Christ....*" I like that terminology. He didn't say, "I was," although, he was. He said, "I am." He said, "I've got a daily recognition that I died with Christ. Nevertheless, I live." I am crucified, yet I'm alive. Yet, not I, but Christ lives in me (Galatians 2:20 paraphrase). Isn't that the mystery of the New Covenant, Christ in us the hope of glory? Us in Him. "*And the life which I now live in the flesh I live by the faith of the Son of God, who loved me, and gave himself for* [there's *for*] *me*" (verse 20, brackets TM). That verse just is overwhelmingly rich! You could just camp out there for a long, long time. Thank you, Jesus. I now live in the flesh by the faith of the son of God, who loved me, and gave himself for me (verse 20 paraphrase).

Even though I am crucified with Christ, I'm alive. Even though I'm alive, it's not me but *Jesus*, the very life of Christ, in me. And I know that if I'm going to be a success in life, I'm going to have to live by faith in the son of God. Hallelujah! The same faith that's working in Him is working in me. There's no different faith. He loves me and gave Himself up for me. And I like this part, "*I do not frustrate the grace of God: for if righteousness come by the law, then Christ is dead in vain*" (Galatians 2:21).

Don't drag me back under the law. Christ did not die in vain. Righteousness cannot come by keeping the law. Righteousness only comes by faith in the grace of God in Christ. Praise God! I got faith in the grace of God in Christ. I receive the grace of God for New Testament living. Hallelujah! I'm not looking back to the old. I'm walking in the new.

Look at Hebrews 10:9. I think it's good to look at some of these to enhance our understanding. You interpret the Word by the Word. The writer of Hebrews said, "*Then said he, Lo, I come to do thy will, O God....* [talking about Jesus]" (Hebrews 10:9, brackets TM). The will of God is the Word of God. The New Testament is the last will and testament of Jesus Christ. Hallelujah! He is the One who gave us the will that engaged us in Him so we can receive the will. He rose from the dead to probate His own will. Praise God! Jesus is alive, not dead. And the Holy Spirit will help us understand the will or the Word of God.

So He said, "*I've come to do your will.*" Then he said this: "*he* [Jesus] *takes away the first that he might establish the second*" (Hebrews 10:9, brackets TM paraphrased). That means He took away the first testament for living (not for learning—you can learn, but don't live there). And He established the second, which is the New Testament, for living.

Look at verse 10, "*By the which will* [by the New Testament, by the blood of Jesus] *we are sanctified through the offering of the body of Jesus Christ once for all*" (brackets TM).

How many people are working hard to be sanctified? You don't have to work hard to be sanctified. You believe the Bible, believe in the blood.

The word *sanctified* means "to make holy." Somebody says, "Well, holiness comes from right living." Listen, I believe in right living, but **right living is a product of right believing**. Hallelujah! It's not just something you tack on that you can say, "I'm righteous because I did this. I did this." Wait a minute; what about what Jesus did? Jesus cleansed us from our sin.

This verse said that through the New Testament blood of Jesus we are sanctified forever, once for all (Hebrews 10:10). Now that settles it. It's nice to get closer to God, grow in your relationship with God, know more about God, hear from God, grow more mature in God—that's all part of Christian growth—but let me tell you something. Sanctification comes through the blood of Jesus.

The word means to make holy. It means to set apart, to consecrate, which means to consecrate to Him, to free from sin, and, I love this one, to qualify for spiritual blessing. I tell you, I'm qualified. *Jesus* qualified me. I'm qualified by the blood of the Lamb. Praise God, Hallelujah! We are set apart as His own. We are chosen in Him before the foundation of the world. Ephesians 1:4 tells us we are chosen in Him. There's an *in Him*. I am chosen in him before the foundation of the world, that we should be holy and without blame before him in love (Ephesians 1:4 paraphrased).

How rich is that love? How good is that love? How great is that love? It's out of sight. I mean, it's way out beyond your natural ability to conceive. You can only receive it by faith and only through the help of the Holy Spirit can you begin to get a grip and a grasp on it.

In one of the Apostle Paul's prayers in the book of Ephesians, he prayed that we may come to know the height, the length, the depth, and the width of the love of God, listen, which passes understanding (see Ephesians 3:18-19). How am I going to know the love of God? Through the help of the Holy Spirit. And He said as you come to know the height, length, depth, and width of the love of God, which passes understanding, you and I can become a people flooded with God himself (Ephesians 3:18-19, AMPC paraphrased).

Do you know what it means to flood? It means beyond your capacity to contain. That's a flood. Would you like to be flooded with God! Hallelujah! Flooded with love! Chosen in Him to be holy and without blame before Him in love (Ephesians 1:4 paraphrased). You are chosen in Him.

PERFECTED IN CHRIST

Let's go back to Hebrews and jump ahead to 10:14, "*For by one offering he hath perfected* [this is Jesus] *for ever them that are sanctified*" (brackets TM). There, it said it again—we are sanctified. We are perfected forever in Christ. Praise the Lord.

He took all of our sin, all of our shame, all of our guilt, and all of our condemnation. There's zero condemnation. We're perfected in Christ. In God's mind, He sees us in Christ. He also perfects us by the New Birth, giving us everything we need. Every part is perfect for us to grow into a full God-man or woman. So don't let the devil condemn you when Jesus made you right. He took our sin at Calvary. He turned the darkness into light. I'm sanctified forever by the blood of the Lamb. Called to walk in victory, I'm a child of the great I AM!

Look at verse 16. He says this, "*This is the covenant* [this is God talking] *I will make with them after those days, saith the Lord.*" So He's talking about the New Covenant now. "*I will put my laws into their hearts and in their minds will I write them*" (verse 16). Well, what law is that? The law of love!

Did you know the love of God is shed abroad in your heart by the Holy Spirit? Hallelujah! Glory to God! Thank you, Jesus. Amen. That's a good one to confess. That's an *in Christ* reality that never could happen before—the love of God shed abroad in our heart.

We're going to be head-to-toe filled with the life and love of God in our hearts, in our minds, in our mouths, in our feet, in our walk, in our talk, in our living, and in our giving. Hallelujah!

Don't miss verse 17: "*And their sins and iniquities will I remember no more.*" Do you see why I say there is zero condemnation in Christ? The devil is a big fat zero because Jesus brought him to nothing. And condemnation has no place in you or in me. So get rid of that guilty feeling. See yourself in the mirror of the Word. See Christ in you in that mirror. Begin to acknowledge every good thing that's in you in Christ. And watch what the Holy Spirit will do. If God doesn't remember my iniquities and my sins, if God doesn't remember any of that, I'm not going to focus on it. Hallelujah! Thank you, Jesus. Amen.

I've made mistakes. I've been born again many years, but I tell you what, the more I know about Jesus, the more I know I'm forgiven, the more I know Jesus, the more I know He lifts me up. He doesn't push me down.

CONDEMNATION VS CONVICTION

Condemnation and conviction are two different things. Conviction draws you to the Lord. Condemnation pushes you away. Conviction gives you hope that God loves you. Yeah, I made a mistake, but I can run to Him. I'm convicted of that.

I said something just recently that I was convicted about. I felt bad about it. But I was drawn *to* God. The devil tries to use the same thing to push you down, make you feel ugly, lost, and worthless. But God is always saying, "Come on. Lift up your eyes. Lift up your heart. Lift up your hands. Receive what My Son's blood has provided."

So know the difference between conviction and condemnation. Conviction draws you to God. Condemnation pushes you away. Conviction is about a particular sin—a certain thing God wants to talk with you about. Condemnation is general, just a general bad feeling about yourself.

So I'm not going to be condemned. When I do make a mistake, I run to Jesus, not from Jesus. I come boldly to the throne of grace. What do you think it's there for? To find help in the time of need, whatever that need is. If it's the need for forgiveness, or the need for strength, or the need for an answer to prayer, or the need for insight, or the need for wisdom, you can come boldly.

Look at Hebrews 10:20, "*By a new and living way, which he* [talking about Jesus] *hath consecrated for us, through the veil, that is to say, his flesh* [his body]" (brackets TM). When the veil was torn in two, from top to bottom, God moved out of the box and came into your heart.

Jesus' body was torn from top to bottom. Christ represents that veil; that veil represents Him. He said, "And having an high priest over the house of God...." He's a faithful and merciful High Priest, by the way. He's faithful to always treat you with mercy when you come to Him.

Hebrews 10:22-23 continues, "*Let us draw near with a true heart in full assurance of faith, having our hearts sprinkled from an evil conscience, and our bodies washed with pure water. Let us hold fast the profession of our faith without wavering; (for he is faithful that promised).*"

Well, that sums it up right there. There's no condemnation in that picture. No guilty feeling in that picture. No strong disapproval there. He said you come boldly with a true heart full of assurance that God loves you and God wants you. Come! He said He'll sprinkle your heart. He'll sprinkle and get rid of all the evil thoughts and condemning thoughts. You'll be washed pure and clean through the precious blood of Jesus. And you can lift your voice and say, "I believe God. I believe His promise. Jesus is Lord. I am forgiven, and the gates of hell cannot prevail against me. I am in Christ!" Hallelujah! Praise God!

ABBA FATHER

I wanted to get to that portion of Hebrews because it's so important to us to understand God's attitude toward condemnation. Now we'll go back to Romans chapter eight.

Romans 8:5 says, "*For you have not received the spirit of bondage again to fear. But you have received the Spirit of adoption, whereby we cry, Abba, Father.*" Hallelujah! It's not a spirit of bondage, but a spirit of sonship. He uses the word "adoption." We're members of the family. We have received a spirit of adoption or inheritance. We have not received the spirit of bondage that causes us to fear, but a spirit of faith that causes us to rejoice. Hallelujah! Glory to God.

Abba is an endearing term. It means "Daddy," Daddy God. God is my Daddy in Christ. He lives in me. Jesus is our elder brother. He's the first born among many brethren. I am in the family. He is our Father. We are His children.

It says in verse 16, "*The Spirit itself* [Himself] *beareth witness with our spirit, that we are the children of God*" (brackets TM). Hallelujah! "*And if children, then heirs...*" (verse 17), heirs of God and joint-heirs *with*—there's that little word, *with*—I'm identified *with* Christ. If He's a joint-heir, I'm a joint-heir. If He's an heir of God, I'm an heir of God.

Did you know Hebrews 1 said that Jesus is the heir and rightful owner of everything? That means that He upholds, maintains, and propels the universe with His mighty Word of power, and we are in Him. Can you get a glimpse of how deep and broad and wide this redemption is? **We will be forever understanding who we are in Christ.** I don't think it stops when we get to heaven. I think we're going to find out more when we get there. But I'm going to keep pressing toward the mark for the prize of the high calling of God in Christ Jesus.

I wrote this song:

"Abba Father.
Daddy God.
Great Physician.
Greater One.
Extreme Deliverer,
Our High Priest.

Abba Father,

Prince of Peace."

Wherever you are as you read this, why don't you just take a moment and thank Him for loving you? Thank Him for showing Himself strong on your behalf. Thank Him for including you, in Christ, in the family. Call Him Daddy God, Abba Father.

HE GIVES US ALL THINGS

We're heirs of God and joint heirs with Christ. Romans 8:17 continues, "*...if so be that we suffer with him, that we may be also glorified together.*" There's another *with* in there—suffer *with* Him. That means our identity *with* Him in His death, burial, and resurrection. We don't suffer sickness and disease with Him because He doesn't have any. The enemy may try to attack you, but you go back to what He suffered for us on the cross—by His stripes, we're healed. And we are with Him in that, so therefore, healing is ours. Praise God.

Remember, when it says we suffer with Him, it doesn't mean we've got to take stripes and go through hell on earth—Jesus already did that. It just simply means that we identify with what He did for us on the cross—what it meant for us—and we claim the result of that. We stand steady under the pressure of temptation, tests, and trials based on the fact that Jesus is alive and we are alive in Him. That's who I am. That's what I have.

So don't act like a beggar. Don't act like a worm. You're a joint-heir with Jesus! The winds may be blowing, the pressure starting to rise. But you just dance and shout and sing and take the devil by surprise! I'm talking about a life of no condemnation. A life of being an heir, a life of victory, and a life of praise and worship and thanksgiving, because you've learned to acknowledge who you are in Christ. Trouble may come, but God is with us. And we have been given the victory. Glory be to God. Hallelujah!

"*What shall we then say to these things?*" it says in Romans 8:31, "*If God be for us, who can be against us?*" Verse 32 goes on, "*He that spared not his own Son, but delivered him up for us all, how shall he not with him also freely give us all things?*" Now catch this: "*Who shall lay anything to the charge of God's elect? It is God that justifies you. Who is he that condemneth?*" (verse 33-34, paraphrased).

No condemnation. Zero condemnation. "*It is Christ that died* [for you], *yea rather, that is risen again, who is even at the right hand of God, who also maketh intercession for you. Who or what shall separate us from the love of Christ? Shall tribulation, distress, persecution, famine, nakedness, peril, problem, sword, wind, or waves.*" (verse 34-35, paraphrased).

We find the answer in verse 37: "*Nay, in all these things we are more than conquerors through him that loved us. For I am persuaded, that neither death, nor life, nor angels, nor principalities, nor powers, nor things present, nor things to come, nor height, nor depth, nor any other creature, shall be able to separate me from the love of God, which is in Christ Jesus my Lord*" (verses 37-39, paraphrased). Hallelujah!

I'm free from guilt and shame. I'm standing in the power of Jesus' name. There is *zero condemnation* for those who are in Christ Jesus.

CHAPTER 11:

TOTAL VICTORY

We are going to start this chapter on victory by looking at what 2 Corinthians chapter two can tell us about our new creation realities. I know we've said a lot about that already, but I want to talk about it some more because in the world you will have tribulation. Jesus said, "*But be of good cheer. I've overcome it for you*" (John 16:33, paraphrased).

I have mentioned that we really have victory guaranteed by the blood of Jesus. It may not come just like you thought it would, and it may not come at the time you think it should, but it'll come. It'll come if we'll stand on the promises of God, listen to the Holy Spirit, and walk by faith and love.

Our Scripture says, "*Now thanks be unto God, which always causeth us to triumph in Christ, and maketh manifest the savour* [or fragrance] *of his knowledge by us in every place*" (2 Corinthians 2:14 brackets TM).

Now, that is such a powerful word, and I just want to point out a couple of things. Number one, let's look at the phrase, "*make manifest the fragrance of His knowledge.*" We're after the knowledge of God. And when you find the knowledge of God, it changes everything. What did God mean when He said what He said? What did God accomplish when He did what He did?

Well, it was done *for* us. I told you of the note I wrote down about the English language not being constructed for prepositions to carry the weight that the Gospel demands they carry. This one says *in Christ* God makes us always to triumph. So His knowledge will give us perfect peace, perfect joy, and complete victory. God did not leave any stone unturned, any sin uncovered, anything missing, or anything broken in our redemption. We just simply pursue God and allow the Holy Spirit to help us and teach us and strengthen us and bring us into the full stature of the fullness of Christ. Hallelujah!

So he said, "*Now thanks be unto God, which always causeth us to triumph.*" I am triumphant in Christ. And I love the phrase *causes us*. That means to me that God gets involved in your situation. I mean, once we release our faith in Him, He goes to work to perform His Word. He's the performer; we're the believer. If I dare believe, God will find a way. Praise God. Hallelujah!

So that brings some peace to me. I am triumphant in Christ. His victory is my victory. I get what He got. I am who He says I am. If He says I'm victorious, then I am victorious!

The old gospel song "Victory In Jesus" tells us He plunged us to victory. I just wrote down in my notes, "I've been dunked!" I'm like a chocolate covered donut—I've been dunked into victory. I'm a victory-covered new creature in Christ Jesus. I've been dunked in the cleansing flood of the blood of the Lamb. I've been saturated with victory, head to toe! I'm clothed in His righteousness. Praise God. Hallelujah!

So right in the middle of the issue, I'm going to praise the Lord. It may not look good, but I'm going to praise the Lord because I know victory is on the way. Despite the words and the chatter of the enemy and the circumstance, I'm going to praise the Lord. Though the enemy may surround me like a swarm, in God's hands I'm safe and warm. Cuz even the bees got to bow their knees when I praise the Lord! Hallelujah!

Victory comes our way. So I praise Him for the victory. I praise Him for His love. I praise Him for His mercy. I praise Him that I am in Christ today made full. Yet I have lots of room to grow. I'm declaring that I'm made full because as I acknowledge every good thing in me that's in Christ, the communication of my faith becomes effectual, and I grow into the Jesus-man that I'm called to be. I've come to the fullness of life. I've been given the victory in Christ Jesus.

THE SMELL OF VICTORY

Go back to our verse; it says, "*Now thanks be unto God, which always causeth us to triumph, and makes manifest the fragrance*" (paraphrased). Victory has a fragrance, and so does defeat. But the fragrance of victory is oh, so, sweet! And that's the fragrance that we are actually manifesting through our knowledge of Christ and who He is. And this works in every place, on every circumstance, and in every situation.

The word "triumph" in that verse is only used twice in the New Testament. The term really is "via triumphalis." It was used by the Romans in those days to parade the conqueror that came back from war. He was paraded down the street of the city, like of Rome, in a celebrity manner. Lots of people would line the streets. The conqueror was in front. Behind him were his warriors and military people who fought with Him. And at the very end of the parade were some of the enemies, usually with the defeated king in chains, and all stripped of their clothing. They had to march humiliated as the conquered in the conqueror's parade. It was called the "via triumphalis," which means "the way of victory."

"Triumph" is a noisy celebratory procession or a parade. He said, "Thanks be unto God who causes us to march in a parade of victory in Christ." It's a parade that proclaims victory, that gives triumphant sounds, and that is a celebration in nature. It's a noisy procession. People are happy, and the picture of this word "triumph" is a conqueror's parade, or a victor's parade like the World Series in baseball. When they win the World Series, a few days later they have a parade in their hometown. And *this* is how God made us to triumph! Praise God. Hallelujah! Thank you, Jesus. Amen.

So when he says God causes us to triumph, we're in the parade as part of the team—the body of Christ. We're also celebrating like the people watching the parade. We're celebrating Jesus! We're celebrating victory! We're celebrating the blood of the Lamb! We're rejoicing.

The word "fragrance" comes from the Roman *via triumphalis* parade; there would be people everywhere, usually on the balconies or up on the hills, and they would be throwing petals of flowers all over the army and the conqueror and the road itself. And there would be a fragrance that would rise up from all those flowers. And it was known as the "fragrance of the via triumphalis." It was the sweet smell of victory. Praise God!

And so we are to raise our voices in praise and adoration to the Lord and be that fragrance, day in and day out, because our victory is complete. It's not just for the World Series or one Super Bowl. It is for all time, for all men and all women, forever!

It might be time for you to join the parade. It might be time for you to have your own parade, just parade around your room.

Praise God! Parade, stomp, and romp, and shout, and dance, and praise the Lord. Hallelujah! He has caused you to triumph and given you the victory!

My youngest daughter was born on Christmas day. When she was just young, maybe five or six years old, I saw her one day outside. She was marching with a stick like she was just marching with a baton or something. And I said, "Honey, what are you doing? Playing parade?"

She said, "Daddy, I *am* the parade!" I thought, *Yeah, you "am" the parade! You "am" the parade!*

Well, you "*am*" the parade too! You're in the parade as part of the team because His victory was for you and me. So we can march in the parade. We can also rejoice because of the parade. And don't forget, at the end of that *via triumphalis* was the defeated king or captain or something, who was in chains, stripped naked, humiliated, and defeated. And that's the very thing the Bible said that Jesus did to the enemy. It says He *spoiled* him. That means to strip one of his title and authority. Hallelujah! Get a new picture of your life. Get a new picture of the enemy. Get a new picture of Christ. See yourself in that parade, and this Scripture comes alive. No wonder it says, "*Now thanks be unto God who causes us to triumph.*" Praise God! Hallelujah!

Let the fragrance flow through your lips. Let the fragrance flow through your mouth. Fill the air with the praises and the thanksgiving and the worship of God. Remember, Jesus conquered death. He conquered the devil. He conquered sin. He conquered guilt. He conquered disease. He conquered debt. He conquered depression. And He did it for us. His victory was our victory. So let's march and let's celebrate. Let's sing and rejoice because God causes us to triumph in Christ Jesus.

It also says in 2 Corinthians 2:14 that it is "always," and "in every place." That means this works on every occasion. We've got Jesus for every occasion. We've got redemption for every occasion. Listen, I know sometimes life can be challenging. Life can be hard. But in the midst of that, we've got Jesus for every occasion. Refuse to fear, and march in the parade. Glory to God! Hallelujah!

In 1 Corinthians 15:57 it says this: "*But thanks be to God, which giveth us the victory through our Lord Jesus Christ.*" Both Scriptures talk about thanking God right in the middle of the matter; we're to begin to praise the Lord. Thanks be to God, which gives us the victory through our Lord Jesus Christ.

Because of this, "*Therefore, my beloved brethren, be ye stedfast, unmoveable, always abounding in the work of the Lord, forasmuch as ye know that your labour* [in God] *is not in vain in the Lord*" (verse 58, brackets TM).

God never sleeps. God never slumbers. He's a rewarder of those who diligently seek Him. And as you're seeking God and trusting Him and marching in the parade, and giving Him glory for the victory, He brings it to pass. God gives us the victory, and God causes us to triumph.

We operate our faith in Him, through His life in us, through His Word, through His counsel, and by His Spirit. We're living in Christ in relationship with Him and what He did. Through Christ and in Christ, I always have the victory.

MADE ALIVE TOGETHER WITH CHRIST

Now, let's go over to Colossians and see the other place that this word "triumph" is used.

Colossians 2:13 is God talking to us: "*And you, being dead in your sins and the uncircumcision of your flesh, hath he quickened together with him* [Christ]..." (brackets TM). I love that terminology, "*quickened together.*" We were all raised with Christ at the same time. You may have accepted it at a different time than I did, but it all happened at the same time. We were quickened together with Christ. We identify with Christ in His resurrection, and He has forgiven us all our trespasses.

"*Blotting out the handwriting of ordinances that was against us, which was contrary to us, and took it out of the way, nailing it to his cross*" (Colossians 2:14). That means all of your sins and circumstances and situations have been taken care of by the precious blood of Jesus Christ. No wonder we can say, "*In Him we live and move and have our being*" (Acts 17:28). Hallelujah! Something happens when we are in Christ that changes everything because something happened in Christ that changed everything.

"*And having spoiled principalities and powers, he made a shew of them openly, triumphing over them in it* [or, in Himself]" (verse 15, brackets TM). Praise God! That's the second place in the New Testament that word "triumph" is used. He triumphed over them in the victory parade. Hallelujah to God! He made us alive together with Christ. He spoiled our enemy. The very life of God is in us.

I love that old song,

"I've got the life of God in me.
His life, His nature, and ability."

Hallelujah! Jesus initiated something—set it in motion, the origination of something, the formal beginning of something—and then he stripped the devil. He just didn't make us alive and leave our enemy big, ugly, and strong. He left him ugly and *defeated.*

The word "*spoiled*" means to divest wholly of one's property, title, and authority. In other words, He stripped the devil of everything he had. He whipped him and stripped him and left him barren.

Visualize our enemy in that parade, bound by chains, naked, humiliated. Jesus said in the book of Revelation, "*I am He that was dead, and now I am alive, and I've got the keys!*" (Revelation 1:18, paraphrase) Hallelujah! He's got the keys of death, hell, and the grave. The devil doesn't have the keys. The devil cannot defeat you. The devil is under our feet. And if we stand up as a new man in Christ Jesus, he will flee from us in absolute terror!

Did you know that word there *flee*—"*Resist the devil, and he will flee from you*" (James 4:7) means "to run as in terror." And then it says this, "as if when someone's hair stands on end." The devil goes, "Waaaaa!! I gotta get out of here!" He says, "Those guys know who they are in Christ! I can't fool with them. Christ has already busted my head once! I never got over that! After 2,000 years, it's still sore!" Hallelujah!

It said He spoiled principalities, and I like this part of verse 15, "*made a shew of them openly.*" The word *shew* ("show") there again talks about a parade. It has that context. The word actually means "to exhibit or to make an open example." And in some cases, a public example, a public exhibit for all to see. The word *exhibit* means "to expose to view." So when it said Jesus made a shew of the enemy, He exposed him for all to see. You've got to get the vision and the image. We need to see what God sees. When we see ourselves in Christ, our eyes start to open up, and we see the enemy from Christ's view. The enemy will flee from you when you see him from the "in Christ" view! Praise God. Hallelujah! Thank you, Jesus. Amen!

Jesus' victory was not done in a back alley somewhere. It was done on a hill for all to see—a place called Mt. Calvary. You can believe it, or you can reject it. But nevertheless, that cross was a dividing line for life. Through the cross, there's life. Reject it, you're in Adam. Receive it, you're in Christ. He made a show of the enemy openly, in Christ, in that victory parade. Praise God! Hallelujah! Glory to God!

GOD'S CENTERPIECE

Did you know the center chapter in the Bible is Psalm 117? It's also the shortest chapter in the Bible. "*O praise the Lord, all ye nations: praise him, all ye people. For his merciful kindness is great toward us: and the truth of the Lord endureth for ever. Praise ye the Lord.*" In those two verses, there are simply three things I'd like us to see.

We're told to, "*Praise the Lord, all ye people, praise him all ye nations, for his merciful kindness is great toward us, and the truth of the Lord endures forever. Praise ye the Lord*" (Psalm 117 paraphrased). The three things I want you to see are praise, mercy, and truth. That's the center of the Bible—praise, mercy, and truth. God put that there for a reason. He said our life ought to be filled with praise, mercy, and truth.

I know there are lots of other things in the Bible, but those are the main things in the center of the Bible. And by the way, the "praise" words in there are two different Hebrew words. One is *halal*, which means "celebrate." The other one is *shabach*, which means "shout unto God with a voice of triumph." Christianity is a celebration of life. Christianity is a celebration of love.

Christianity is a celebration of who we are in Christ by His grace through faith. Praise the Lord. Glory to God. Hallelujah!

Remember my story from earlier in the book about the big guy yelling in the praise service? He'd been left for dead, but God brought him back around and gave him another chance, and turned him on to Jesus! He could have lost his life and gone to hell; he was that close. But ever since he came out of that coma, he just felt such a love of God swell up in him that once in a while in a praise service he'll just go, "Yeaaahh!"

So, once in a while when I'm preaching or teaching somewhere, I say, "Why don't we all try it right now. Everybody go, "Yeeeahhh!" Maybe you want to do that at home or wherever you're at, "Yeeeaahhh!" Because the new creation life is a celebration of what Jesus has done! He is the way, the truth, and the life. No man comes to the Father but by Him, but anybody can come. And when we come to Christ, we not only get our sins remitted, but we become new creatures. We get out of Adam and get into Christ; He fills us and He floods us with the power of His promise, the power of His spirit, and He gives us a song to sing. He says, "My victory is your victory. Get in the parade with Me and rejoice in what I've done for you." And once we start living life that way, things will come in line. Praise God. Hallelujah!

YOUR FOE IS DEFEATED

The Bible tells us Jesus spoiled principalities. Again, to *spoil* means "to strip or dispossess one of his property, titles, and authority." So the devil has been stripped and whipped. He's busted and broken. His head has been bruised, and Jesus is Lord.

Don't take any junk from the devil. Use the name of Jesus and bind him; cast him out. Take dominion over him. The Bible tells us to give him no place. The Bible tells us to resist him, and he will flee from us. The Bible tells us to be sober and vigilant because he's roaming around trying to find somebody to pick on. Don't let him pick on you. You remember that Jesus was manifested to destroy the works of the devil (1 John 3).

In 1 John 3:8 it says this: "*He that committeth sin is of the devil; for the devil sinneth from the beginning. For this purpose the Son of God was manifested, that he might destroy the works of the devil.*" That word *destroy* means "to dissolve." It means to loosen or to melt down. Jesus melts down the bondages of sin. He melts down the bondages that have held people captive. He sets people free through His blood and by His name. That word means "to loose, or dissolve, or take off, or reduce to constituent particles." In other words, God said Jesus came to absolutely pulverize, to reduce to powder, the works of darkness. So every time the devil raises his ugly head, take the name of Jesus and hit him again!

Look with me at 1 John 5:1-3: "*Whosoever believeth that Jesus is the Christ is born of God: and every one that loveth him that begat loveth him also that is begotten of him. By this we know that we love the children of God, when we love God, and keep his commandments. For this is the love of God, that we keep his commandments: and his commandments are not grievous.*" They're not grievous; they're for our good. "*But whosoever is born of God overcometh the world*" (verse 4 paraphrase). That's pretty plain, isn't it? The seed of God Himself, the seed of the life of God, is in us. The seed of the victory of Christ is in us. The seed of the righteousness of God is in us. We overcome the world. Hallelujah! Jesus said I've overcome the world for you, so if I'm born of God, I get what He got. I get what He is. "*And this is the victory that overcometh the world, even our faith*" (verse 4). Praise God!

Faith is important. Believing God. Trusting God's Word. Standing on His promise. Believing and speaking and acting like the Bible's true—all these things are important. Our faith in God, our faith in Christ, guarantees our victory. The devil is a liar, and that liar's going in the lake of fire.

Look at verse 5, "*Who is he that overcometh the world, but he that believeth that Jesus is the Son of God*?" Hallelujah! I qualify for victory in every area of life. How about you? I am an overcomer through faith in Jesus. Hallelujah!

Did you know that Word *overcome* in the Greek means "to subdue, to prevail against, to conquer, to overcome, or to get the victory"? Hallelujah! It comes from the Greek word *nike*. Have you ever heard of Nike shoes? That's where they got that, *nike*. *Nike* means to overcome. The word *nike* means to be victorious. It means success or victory. Praise God. Hallelujah! Thank you, Jesus. Amen.

Sometimes I just buy something that has the Nike swish on it because I know it means "overcomer." I know it's a scriptural word. I'm not saying the company is scriptural. I don't know anything about them. I'm just telling you where they got the name.

This is a victory that knocks out the world, knocks out the devil, and knocks out the flesh. It knocks out fear. This is the victory that overcomes the world, even our faith. This is the victory that can cause us to succeed—knowing who we are in Christ. Knowing what He did and what He made us to be affects you and me. We are more than conquerors in Christ. In Him, we have the victory. In Him, we have *nikaó-d* the world and the devil and the flesh. In Him we have *nike*. We have success because of what He did and who He is.

YOU ARE THE FRAGRANCE OF CHRIST

I want to go back to 2 Corinthians 2:14 in the light of everything else we've learned in this chapter: "*Now thanks be unto God, which always causeth us to triumph in Christ, and maketh manifest the savour* [or the fragrance] *of his knowledge by us in every place.*" (brackets TM).

I like verse 15 in the Amplified. It says, "*For we are the sweet fragrance of Christ.*" Praise God. Remember, when our faith becomes effectual, we will share it. Somebody's going to see Jesus in me. Somebody's going to see Jesus in you. And in this case, somebody's going to pick up a "scent" that there's something different about you. They'll smell something. It smells good. They're not sure what it is, but boy, it smells good! You're always joyful. You've always got a smile on your face. You're always rejoicing. They know you're going through a hard time—you just lost your job or something, but you're still happy. That is the victory of Christ in your life and in my life! They'll smell it on you!

Remember my song says, "*Don't smell like defeat.*" It's a Jamaican song.

"*Don't smell like defeat. Smell like the head.*"

What does that mean? Don't smell like defeat. Smell like the head. Well, who's the head? Christ. We're the fragrance of the Christ. How am I going to do that? By acknowledging every good thing that's in me in Christ Jesus, by getting in the victory parade, having a little parade every day or every so often.

Aren't you glad you belong to the household of God? And aren't you glad you belong in the victory parade? Aren't you glad you belong to Him?

We have been given victory in Christ Jesus. No doubt about it. It belongs to us through His blood. It belongs to us by His name. It belongs to us according to His plan and purpose for us. He initiated a whole new system. It's initiated by His blood. It's a system of victory. It's a system of completeness. It's a system of peace. It's ours today. He set it in motion. Praise God! We are New Covenant believers. We live in the New Covenant. We learn from the old, but we live in the new. God has put Satan and his defeat on display. And the victory of Christ is ours today.

CROSS ON OVER

Remember to think about that when you face the problems of life. Don't look at the problem from the problem's side. Look at the problem from the victory side! **"Cross" on over and look back at the problem through the eyes of faith.** Through the eyes of faith, you can see what God sees. Through the eyes of faith, you can have what Jesus provided.

We can walk in a new realm of victory and peace, joy and love, and carry out God's plan to the full extent by knowing Jesus. In Him we live and move and have our being. The Holy Spirit has come to help us. We're not alone. Remember that. It's not just about knowing the Word. It is about knowing the Word, but not *just* about knowing the Word. It's about knowing the Holy Spirit and allowing Him to lead us and to guide us and to help us and to strengthen us. And, I tell you right now, He'll get right in your problems with you. The Holy Ghost will celebrate with you. Praise God! Because the Bible said the kingdom of God is righteousness, peace, and joy in the Holy Ghost.

So the Spirit has come to lift us and to fill us and to help us and to reveal Christ to us. It's by His help that we go forward.

Remember, Jesus said, "I will not leave you alone. I will send you another Comforter, and He'll be with you forever." And I love that because we understand that when He comes, He comes in *power*. He comes in wisdom. He comes in strength. He comes in glory. He comes in might, and He lives on the inside of us. Hallelujah! And we can know that the might of God and the Spirit of God is in us today to put us over.

When we think about Him and His place in our lives, He will talk to us about the victory of Christ. He will talk to us about the plan of God. He will talk to us about the ways of God. He will reveal to us the Word of God. Jesus said He will show you things to come. He will help you understand the way. He will fill you with joy each and every day.

He said in the Old Covenant that it's not by might of man or power of man, but it is by the Holy Spirit (Zechariah 4:6). So trust Him. Trust Him to help you. Trust Him to show you. Trust Him to teach you. Trust Him to display the victory of Christ in your life so you can understand and grip it and hold onto it. Believe me, He'll be dancing right with you in the victory parade. Hallelujah!

CHAPTER 12:

IN LOVE IN CHRIST

We've come to our final chapter, and I am so excited to teach you on this subject, Living in Love in Christ. I think this sums everything up because the commandment of the New Testament is the royal law of love. It puts everything together and shows us how to live in Christ in love in Christ.

I'm reminded of that song of mine that simply goes like this:

"Living in Christ, alive, alive, living in God's love.

In heavenly places hid in God, I am far above.

Living in Christ, so God's living in me,

His life, His nature, and ability.

Living in Christ, living God in me, alive, alive, alive."

What a song! And as I was writing that, I just stuck on that one phrase: *Living in Christ, alive, alive, living in God's love.* When talking about living in love in Christ, it ought to certainly be understood that they go together, but many times people do not realize that we can only live in love when we're living in Christ. They want to have the things of God without the character of God or the nature of God. His life, His nature, and ability are in us. His life is eternal. His nature is love. His ability is ours today. And so when we live in love, we live in Christ. And when we live in Christ, we live in love. Remember, love is a new creation reality. Did you ever think about that? That this could not have happened to us without the new creation coming into being. And not only are we made new creatures in Christ, we're made new "*love*" creatures. We are love people of a love God and so we are to walk in love.

We're going to be studying Galatians, so let's get into this teaching. Galatians 5:6 is going to sum up this concept for us: "*For in Jesus Christ neither circumcision availeth any thing, nor uncircumcision; but faith which worketh by love.*"

So it's not about keeping the law. It's not about what you *can* do in the natural or in the flesh, and it's not about what you *can't* do in the flesh. It's not about the color of your skin. It's not about your heritage or your background. It's not about the title that someone may put upon you or in your life. It's not about any of those things—the outside.

It's about an inward working of the Spirit of God—new creation realities of faith in Christ, and this faith works by *love*.

So actually, without the love of God working in us and without us yielding to the love of God, this won't work. Our life in Christ is given to us by a loving Father. And He expects us to walk in His love for us and to let His love shine through us. If we are to express the true new nature of the new you, it must be done in love.

GOD CAN TRUST LOVERS

These are among the words of Jesus—in John 13:34, Jesus said, "*A new commandment I give unto you, That ye love one another; as I have loved you, that ye also love one another.*"

Now that's the new royal commandment of Christ, that we love one another as He has loved us. So in other words, the same love He loves us with, we are to love each other with. Watch this. Verse 35 says, "*By this shall all men know that ye are my disciples, if ye have love one to another.*" Isn't that something? **He said the telltale sign of Christianity is loving one another**—not fighting, not quarrelling, not bickering, not criticizing, not judging, not competing, but loving one another.

And He said people will see it, and all will come to know that this is the love of God in us for each other. We are to be governed by love.

There is such a thing as a love limit in our lives. In other words, God can trust us with revelation knowledge to the level that we are willing to commit to loving. He is not going to put such power in the hands, hearts, minds, and mouths of people who are not committed to walking in love.

The love limit is God's limit in your life. But we don't *have to be limited*, for we can commit to love. And the Bible said we're to pray that God would give us understanding of the height, length, depth, and breadth of the love of God, so that we can be a person flooded with God! Flooded with *in Christ* realities, flooded with the new creation realities that this is who we are because we're in Him, and He's in us, and that love is causing us to overflow with His presence.

So let that love be the force that drives us, or leads us, or causes us to go forward in the things of God. Let that love live big in our lives. Let that love be in our hearts day in and day out. Let that love be in our mouths. Let us use that which God has given us—His Word and His Spirit and His ability—to walk in the love of God.

LOVE IS SHED ABROAD IN OUR HEARTS

Look at Romans 5:1-2, "*Therefore being justified by faith, we have peace with God through our Lord Jesus Christ: By whom also we have access by faith into this grace wherein we stand, and rejoice in hope of the glory of God*" (Romans 5:1-2).

So I'm standing in the grace of God. I'm standing in this sea of right standing. And I'm rejoicing and accessing God's goodness by faith. "*And not only so, but we rejoice in tribulations, also knowing that the tribulation works patience*" (verse 3). Now watch this. "*And patience*, [works] *experience; and experience, hope*: *And hope maketh not ashamed*" (verses 4-5 paraphrased, brackets TM). In other words, our hope will not be disappointed "*because the love of God is shed abroad in our hearts by the Holy Spirit which is given unto us*" (verse 5 paraphrased).

He said this love that was poured out in our hearts by the Holy Spirit is New Testament reality love. It's really a new creation reality because this could never have happened before Jesus came. There's no way that anyone could have the love of God poured into their heart by the Holy Spirit without becoming a new creation. God's not going to pour that kind of love into the old man. The old you can't contain it. The old you can't handle it. The old you isn't ready for it. But in Christ, we're ready for the love of God!

It will fill us up to overflowing. So the love of God has been shed abroad in our hearts by the Holy Spirit. Now, I know that doesn't have, "*in Him, in Christ,* or *in whom*" in that verse, but it's still a new creation reality. And I'd like for you to mark that verse; decree it and acknowledge it. "The love of God is shed abroad in my heart by the Holy Spirit. That's who I am. That's what I have. I have the love of God. I'm a love person. The love of God is shed abroad in my heart."

We can't just talk about it. We've got to walk it out. And when we walk it out, we can have everything that God has provided for us because He can trust us to steward the gifts, the graces, the power, and the mercies of God because we've learned to walk in love.

THE LOVE CHAPTER

Now, let's look at 1 Corinthians 13, which is called the love chapter. Chapter 12 is the chapter on the gifts of the Spirit—the power gifts, the vocal gifts, the operational gifts, the miracle gifts. And I'm telling you, those gifts are dynamic for us as new creation people. They're available to us—the word of wisdom, the word of knowledge, discerning of spirits, the gift of faith, working of miracles, gifts of healings, tongues, interpretation of tongues, and prophecy. All nine of those are available to us, and they are powerful. But he said to desire earnestly the *best* gifts. And he said, "*And yet I show you a more excellent way...*" (1 Corinthians 12:31, paraphrased).

He said when you get over into the love of God and commit to the love commandment, it fulfills the law. Praise God. Hallelujah! He said God can trust us with those power gifts. In ways He could never release them before, they'll be released in our lives because we are new creation individuals who walk in the love of God. That's love shed abroad in my heart by the Holy Spirit.

So let me just read down through 1 Corinthians 13 in the Amplified Bible. It says this: "*If I* [can] *speak in the tongues of men and* [even] *of angels, but have not love (that reasoning, intentional, spiritual devotion such as is inspired by God's love for and in us)....*" Now that's an important thing—it's God's love *for* me and God's love *in* me. So I receive His love. He loved me, and I'm a lover. Hallelujah! He said, "...If I can speak in the tongues of men and angels, and have not love, I am only a noisy gong or a clanging cymbal" (1 Corinthians 13:1 paraphrased).

Over the years, I began to acknowledge this verse, and I would say something like this: "I do speak in the tongues of men and angels, and I do have love." How do I know that? Because it's shed abroad in my heart. "Therefore, I am not a noisy gong or a clanging cymbal." That's true. That's what He said. If I'll yield to love, then I'm not just a noisy gong. I'm not just tooting my horn. I'm not just making noise. I'm lifting up Jesus. I'm loving people. I'm loving you. You're loving me. We're loving Christ. We're reaching the world.

Verse two, "*And if I have prophetic powers (the gift of interpreting the divine will and purpose), and understand all the secret truths and mysteries and possess all knowledge, and if I have [sufficient] faith so that I can remove mountains, but have not love (God's love in me) I am nothing (a useless nobody)*" to the kingdom of God (AMPC). That's pretty heavy, isn't it? So, that puts an importance on this thing called love when we come to new creation realities. Remember, we are a love new creation. We are birthed by God, who is love. The divine seed of His love is in us, shed abroad in our hearts. Let it be. Love like you never loved before.

I often quote and acknowledge this chapter over myself. I say things like, "I do have some prophetic power. I do have some gifts. I do have some faith to remove mountains, but I also have love. Therefore, I am useful to the kingdom of God."

It's not about me or about you in that sense. It's about God getting the glory and His love prevailing. God wants to use all of us in His kingdom in the body of Christ. I don't have to push myself in front of someone. I just love God and let God have His way. I'm happy when someone gets saved, whether I preach the message or not. The angels rejoice if one sinner repents, so it's about love. It's about loving one another. It's about recognizing others. It's about lifting others. It's about being confident in God, who loves you, and letting that love lead you, guide you, and motivate you. If we do that, Paul says that God can use you! You're useful to God in the kingdom. There's a place in the kingdom for those who love!

Now, I know that if you're reading this book you're likely born again and love God, but I'm saying right now we're developing this understanding of new creation realities as unto the love of God that's shed abroad in our heart. And then verse three said, "*Even if I dole out all that I have [to the poor in providing] food, and if I surrender my body to be burned [or in order that I may glory, but have not love (God's love in me), I gain nothing*" (AMPC). It doesn't work.

Did you know you can give your tithe and offering, and if you don't really walk in the love of God, then it will affect your return? It says it will not work. I think many times the devil knows he can stop the flow by getting us in offence, for instance, or unforgiveness. And that's something outside of the love of God. So, I have to guard that very closely. If I get in offence with my wife or someone (or whatever other sin), I try to get it straight as soon as

I can. Because I don't want my offering, I don't want my *life,* to be hindered. And I don't want my giving to fail. I don't want the devil to be able to stop my harvest. I'm going to walk in love. Praise God. Hallelujah!

My giving grows because I love. It's working today. The money will come. Victory is mine. Jesus is Lord. I'm walking in love. I'm letting that love lead me and guide me. I'm letting it be a part of my life. I'm letting it dominate me. I begin to think in love, talk in love, act in love, and reach out in love to touch people in the name of the Lord Jesus Christ.

And then the Amplified begins to describe what love is. Notice it says, "*Love endures long and is patient and kind*" (1 Corinthians 12:4 AMPC). That's pretty good. Sometimes I just get stopped on the first little description of what love is, and I ask, "Am I enduring long, am I patient and kind with others?" God wants me to be.

I don't know about you, but He's been so patient with me. God has been so kind to me. And I want to be kind to people. I want to endure long and be patient and kind and love them. He goes on to say, "*Love never boils over with jealousy, and love is not envious*" (verse 4 AMPC, paraphrased). "*Love is not boastful or vainglorious. It does not brag on itself. It doesn't display itself haughtily*" (verse 4 AMPC, paraphrased). Wow. I mean, love is a humble force, but buddy, it is a force!

"*Love is not conceited, not arrogant, nor inflated with pride; it is not rude, or unmannerly. Love does not act unbecomingly*" (verse 9 AMPC, paraphrased). You know, we can be kind and gracious to one another. You know, sometimes we get upset because somebody made a mistake. Well, I just remember I've made a lot of them. Give people a break; you like to have a break. Show mercy; you want mercy. Show love; you want love. Actively pursue this love, the Bible says. As a matter of fact, it says, "Make this love your great aim and your great quest." New creation reality—the love of God is shed abroad in my heart by the Holy Spirit. I have God's love in me in Christ. That's who I am. That's what I have. Hallelujah!

So it says this, "*Love endures long. It's not conceited, not arrogant, not rude*" (verse 4 AMPC, paraphrased). Don't be rude. It does not act unbecomingly. I love this, "*love does not insist on its own rights or its own way. It is not self-seeking. It is not touchy or fretful or resentful. It takes no account of the evil done to it. It pays no attention to a suffered wrong*" (verse five, paraphrased). Praise God. Hallelujah!

THE AGAPE LOVE OF GOD

Paul is talking about the *agape* love of God. The *agape* love of God is a love by choice, not by feeling or by merit. God didn't love me because I deserved it. He said when I was a sinner, He loved me and died for me. So, the agape love can't be, "I'll love you if you love me. I'll be nice to you if you're nice to me." No. The agape love is a love by choice. I do it by choice; I choose to love people. I choose to love others. I choose to walk in love.

And sometimes, it can be hard on the flesh. If you walk in love, justification will come. Don't always try to find justification from man. Get justification from God. And walk in love. Choose to walk in love. It's not by merit. You know, it's not because somebody deserves it. It's simply because we choose to love like God loves. Hallelujah!

I tell you, when I found that out, it helped me so much to walk in the love of God—not that I'm perfect in myself. But I mean, when I can choose to be kind instead of grumpy, when I can choose to believe the best instead of believe the worst, when I can choose to keep my mouth shut instead of criticizing someone, that's a powerful thing! I can choose to walk in love.

Love is not inflated with pride. It does not act unbecomingly. It's not touchy or resentful or fretful. It takes no account of the evil done to it, pays no attention to a suffered wrong. Have you ever been around somebody where you can just hope they're in a good mood today? Because, when they're in a bad mood, everybody knows it! Well, if that's you quit it! Choose to walk in love.

Walking in the love of God is what's going to put you over and make you successful, because God loved us with that kind of love, and we are to love one another with the same love that Jesus loved us with. Hallelujah! Praise God! There is victory in love. We're more than conquerors through His love, through Him that loved us, and letting that love work in us causes us to walk in super victory in Christ Jesus.

Paul goes on in the "love chapter" to say, "*Love does not rejoice at injustice and unrighteousness, but love rejoices when right and truth prevail*" (1 Corinthians 13:6 AMPC). Hallelujah! Praise God. Amen! That's a good thing. We shouldn't get happy when somebody really gets what they deserve. I'm glad I didn't always get what I deserved! God loved me through thick and thin. He was patient with me.

I was running from God. I was raised in a preacher's home, and I was playing music in nightclubs. But God was just patient with me. Somebody was praying for me. Thank God, He forgave me. Thank God, He reached me. Thank God, He touched my life.

Now, I'm *not* saying that people can run over us all the time and we don't draw a line, have a boundary, or have a standard. I think you can raise a standard in love. Sometimes you have to raise a standard and say, "I love you, but you can't do that here." Just because you love somebody doesn't mean you just let them do what they want to do all the time. Particularly, if they're in your home or in your life or you're dealing with them on a personal basis. It's okay to have boundaries.

But love rejoices when *right and truth* prevail. So we're not just going to let somebody do the wrong thing and get away with whatever in the name of love. We can draw a line, but we do it in a godly way.

We do not seek our own way. We're not touchy, or fretful, or resentful. Love takes no account of the evil done to it; pays no attention to a suffered wrong. Sometimes that may not be easy, but it does pay off. Love does not rejoice at injustice and unrighteousness, but rejoices when right and truth prevail (1 Corinthians 13:6).

The next verse says, "*Love bears up under anything and everything that comes, is ever ready to believe the best of every person, its hopes are fadeless under all circumstances* (That's some kind of power!), *and it endures everything [without weakening]*" (1 Corinthians 13:7 AMPC, parenthesis TM).

Let me tell you something; there is nothing as strong as love. God *is* love. This describes who God is and how He treated us and He looked at us and how He believed the best of us and how He gave the best for us. Hallelujah! **God is love, and that love is shed abroad in my heart, and I'm telling you, that makes me a powerhouse for God.**

It says here that through that love I can bear up under anything. I can get ready for anything. I can believe the best of people, that my hopes will never fade out, and that my hopes and dreams will come to pass. I can endure without weakening.

And then Paul sums it up in verse eight and says, "*Love never fails.*"

Praise God! I like to say, "I never fail!" When we acknowledge this chapter, we use our own pronoun "me"— I never fail. I bear up under anything through the love of God. I'm ready to believe the best of every person through the love of God. My hopes are fadeless under all circumstances through the love of God. And I endure everything without weakening through the love of God. I never fail because God never fails. And God is in me. Love is in me. I'm in Christ. I'm in love. And victory is mine. My giving works. My life is a testimony. My heart stays in tune. And the devil can't stop me. God is for me. I win. Praise God! Hallelujah!

Then verse 13 says, "*And so faith, hope, love abide, these three, but the greatest of these is love*" (AMPC, paraphrased).

PURSUE THIS LOVE

First Corinthians 14:1 in the Amplified Bible tells us, "*Eagerly pursue and seek to acquire [this] love [make it your aim, your great quest]; and earnestly desire and cultivate the spiritual endowments (gifts), especially that you may prophesy....*"

We've talked about being a new creature in Christ, being made the righteousness of God in Christ, being the handiwork of God, living the good life, being alive in Christ, coming out of Adam, coming into Christ, and victory being ours. We've talked about first-class freedom. We've talked about victory in Jesus. We've talked about zero condemnation. And this chapter is to bring no condemnation. It's to bring light and liberty because the love of God is shed abroad in our heart by the Holy Spirit.

God says to all of us: pursue this love. It will keep everything in focus. It will keep everything going the right way. And it will cause us to inherit God's best. Love never fails! Love never fades out. Love never comes to an end. There's victory in the love of God. And that love is in me. That love is in you. And when we allow that love to govern our actions, our words, and our responses, we are going to be on the winning side every time! Not half the time—every time! It'll always turn in the favor of the lover. Praise God. Hallelujah!

The love of God shed abroad in our heart makes the difference in everything. It not only makes life worthwhile and worth living, but it causes life to spring forth. It nurtures life. It nurtures revelation. It causes us to live the way Jesus lived and the way God is, because God is love.

John 3:16 says, "*For God so greatly loved and dearly prized the world that He [even] gave up His only begotten (unique) Son, so that whoever believes in (trusts in, clings to, relies on) Him shall not perish (come to destruction, be lost) but have eternal (everlasting) life*" (AMPC). That whosoever believes in Him—in His love; do you believe God loves you? Well, sure you do. God loves me. Well, that love that He loves you with has been poured out in your heart. I can release that love to my family and my friends. I can release that love in my circumstances and situations. When the Bible says, "*Greater is he that's in us than he that's in the world*" (1 John 4:4), you could say, "Greater is the love of God in me than anything in this world." Hallelujah!

Romans chapter eight says, "*I'm persuaded beyond doubt* (am sure) *that neither death nor life, nor principalities nor powers, nor things present or things to come, not height or depth, nor anything else in all creation can separate me from the love of God which is in Christ Jesus our Lord*" (Romans 8:38-39, paraphrased).

Where is it? In Christ Jesus, my Lord.

When the Apostle Paul said after thirty years of ministry, "I'm trying to get a grip on what got a grip on me," he was talking about getting a grip on this new creation reality of the love of God that had a grip on him and changed his name, set him on the right path, and called him to be the apostle of God that wrote two-thirds of the New Testament. He said, "I want this love living big in me." Hallelujah!

In love and in *Christ* go together. John 3:16 says love is the basis of our redemption.

Ephesians 2:4 says, "*But God, who is rich in mercy, for his great love wherewith he loved us....*" What? The Amplified Bible says, "*But God—so rich is He in His mercy! Because of and in order to satisfy the great and wonderful and intense love....*"

Did you know that God is intensely in love with you and me today? He's greatly in love with you and me today. So much was He in love with us that He wouldn't have it any other way. He said, "I've got to set them free no matter what it cost. It cost Him the life of His son. Praise God, He raised Him from the dead. We were raised with Him, and now we're seated with Him in heavenly places. All because of love! That's powerful stuff. So when I say the love of God is shed abroad in my heart by the Holy Spirit, I'm talking about living in Christ, living in love, and living in new creation realities. Hallelujah!

The love of God is in me! That's who I am. That's what I have. I yield to that love because of "*his great love wherewith he loved us, Even when we were dead in sins, hath quickened us together with Christ, (by grace ye are saved;) And hath raised us up together, and made us sit together in heavenly places in Christ Jesus:* [Now watch this.] *That in the ages to come he might shew the exceeding riches of his grace in his kindness toward us through Christ Jesus*" (Ephesians 2:5-6 brackets TM).

Jesus was the extension of the Father's love. Jesus redeemed us from the curse of the law because He loved us. We are quickened together with Christ by grace, which is a manifestation of love. God so loved the world that He gave His only begotten Son, and that love is in me, and I'm saying to us that as new creatures in a new creation, we need and should acknowledge the good thing that's in us. **Love is a good thing. Love is a great thing. Love is a God thing, and it's in you and me.** Thank God, that's who I am. That's what I have. I'm going to walk in love. I'm going to be a lover—like God, my Father, my Daddy. His love genes are in me. His righteousness genes are in me—His life, His nature, His ability. Hallelujah! I can love. I can forgive. I can forget. I can go forward. Love forgets those things that are behind. Love reaches forward to what's in front. Love presses on toward the mark of the high calling of God in Christ Jesus—or the high calling of love. God is love. The love of God is shed abroad in my heart by the Holy Spirit.

THE LOVE BOOK

So I had it in my heart in this final chapter to talk about *in Love* and *in Christ.* And you'll find those two terms in many Scriptures. They're together because they go together.

When we know who we are in Christ, or in Him, and walk in love, we are absolutely *invincible*, because that's God. That's who God is. He's invincible. He's in us. We're in Him. This is *Living in Christ.* Praise the Lord!

So let's look at the first one where you see it together over in Ephesians 1:3: "*Blessed be the God and Father of our Lord Jesus*

Christ, who hath blessed us with all spiritual blessings [or supernatural blessings] *in heavenly places in Christ*" (brackets TM).

"*According as he hath chosen us* ***in him*** [Christ] *before the foundation of the world....*" Wow! That's a little more than we can handle mentally, but it's still true. Before the foundation of the world, He chose us in Him! Read that again: "*...before the foundation of the world, that we should be holy and without blame before him* ***in love***" (verse 4).

You see those two phrases go together—*in Him, in love*. The love of God has been shed abroad in our hearts by the Holy Ghost because we are *in Him*. So life *in Christ* and life *in love* go together.

God is love. We're talking about *agape* love, which is love by choice. I choose to love. I choose to walk in love. I choose to let love dominate my life. I acknowledge that God's love is in me. I acknowledge that's who I am. I'm a love person from a love God. I'm born of love. I live in love. I have a life in Christ. I may not look like much, but really I'm a lover of God! And I'm a lover of people. That love breaks every barrier. That love can open every door. That love can make all things new. That love forgives. That love sets free. That love causes you and me to be all God's called us to be. God is love, and so are we. The love of God is shed abroad in our hearts.

The entire book of 1 John is a love book. He talks more about love than any other book, it seems to me. We're going to see that this is a book of life, a book of love, and a book of light. We can find ourselves in the life and love of God because we're in Christ. In Him, in love, we are connected. We are love connected. God will never forsake us. God believes the best of us. God sees us in Christ.

Yes, we may slip and fall but get right back over into that realm where love reigns. That's the safety zone. That's the blessing zone.

That's the power zone. He knows when we mess up, but He forgives us. He walks with us. He talks with us. He makes this very clear in the book of 1 John and other places in the Bible that we are responsible to let this love dominate our actions and our attitudes. Praise God!

Ephesians 3:20 says that God is able to do far over and above all we dare ask or think according to the power that works in us. And part of that power is love power. Faith power is in there; I understand that. Holy Ghost power is in there. But love power is a big part of the power that is available to the new creation in Christ. When you've got faith power, Holy Ghost power, and love power, God says, "I can do far over and above all you can dare even ask or think." Praise God!

So, I don't know about you, but as for me, I'm going to pursue life in the Kingdom. I'm going to pursue life in love. And I'm going to pursue life in Christ because I'm a new creature. I'm living in a new creation reality through Jesus Christ and God's great love.

So look with me in 1 John 2:3. Now you're going to see *in Him* and *in love* in these verses, so they go together: "*And hereby we do know that we know him, if we keep his commandments.*"

Well, we just read His commandment—Jesus' New Testament commandment is a commandment of love. Remember, Jesus said, "Here's the commandment, love the Lord your God with all your heart, soul, mind, and strength, and your neighbor as yourself. And then love one another as I have loved you" (paraphrased). So we are to love one another. There's not a whole lot of God's love in some people. It's all about selfish love, that selfish realm of what I can get for myself, and forget about everybody else. But God's love is greater than that.

So John said, "*And hereby we do know that we know him, if we keep his commandments*" (1 John 2:3). Verse four, "*He that saith, I know him, and keepeth not his commandments, is a liar,* [liar, liar pants on fire] *and the truth is not in him*" (brackets TM). You can't just say, "Well, I'm a new creature in Christ," and then not walk in love toward your fellow believer.

"*But whoso keepeth his word, in him verily* [truly] *is the love of God perfected; hereby know we that we are in him*" (1 John 2:5, brackets TM).

This is an *in Him* reality that's going to be manifested through the love of God that's in our heart.

"*He that saith he abideth in him ought himself also so to walk, even as he walked*" (verse 6). Jump ahead to verse eight, "*Again, a new commandment I write unto you, which thing is true in him and in you.*" What? He said this love commandment is already in you because the darkness is past, and the true light is shining (verse 8).

"*He that saith he is in the light, and hateth his brother, is in darkness.... He that loveth his brother abideth in the light, and there is none occasion of stumbling in him*" (verses 9-10 paraphrased). When we walk in love, there's no way we can stumble. We're always going to get up. If we do trip, we go forward instead of backward because the love of God is shed abroad in our hearts by the Holy Ghost.

First John chapter three says we have a manner of love that is from God, and that is what distinguishes us as sons of God—this love of God that's shed abroad in our hearts. The greater One is in us. That greater One is love.

THE LOVE OF GOD

Let's go over to the 1 John 4 as we begin to close this chapter with this thought about love. Look with me in chapter four and verse seven, "*Beloved, let us love one another: for love is of God; and every one that loveth is born of God, and knoweth God. He that loveth not knoweth not God; for God is love. In this was manifested the love of God toward us, because that God sent his only begotten Son into the world, that we might live through him*" (1 John 4:7-9) There's that preposition *through*.

John goes on, "*Herein is love, not that we loved God, but that he loved us, and sent his Son to be the propitiation for our sins. Beloved, if God so loved us, we ought also to love one another. No man hath seen God at any time. If we love one another, God dwelleth in us, and his love is perfected in us. Hereby know we that we dwell in him...*" (1 John 4:12-14).

I'm in Him. How do I know that? When I love the brethren. When I let this love dominate my life, my thinking, my actions, and my attitude. When I learn to forgive and release and pray for people, and lift people, and love people by choice. I know problems come, pain comes, and hurt comes, but release them through the love of God. Let love heal and help you display the character of Christ like never before.

"*Hereby know we that we dwell in him, and he in us, because he hath given us of his Spirit*" (1 John 4:13). We know we dwell in Him because He dwells in us.

Look down at verse number 16, "*And we have known and believed the love that God hath to us. God is love; and he that dwelleth in love dwelleth in God, and God in him.*"

That's it! If we're going to live in a new creation reality, we're going to have to be dominated by the love of God. Let it live big in me. It's a good thing. It's a God thing. It's a great thing.

Verse 17, "*Herein is our love made perfect, that we may have boldness in the Day of Judgment: because as he is, so are we in this world.*" As He is, so are *we* in this world. God is love! *We* are love! We are New Testament believers. We are in the new creation realities. And that reality is that God loves me, and I'm going to love you, and I'm going to let that love dominate me, and it will see me through. Victory is mine each and every day, and there really is no other way but to walk in the love of God. The greater One will come through. Victory will be your portion, and all things will work together for good to them that love God because God's love is shed abroad in our hearts.

WE CARRY THIS REALITY

Throughout the course of this book, we have followed the markers in the Word—these seemingly small prepositions—that show us who we are in, with, for, and by Christ. These little words are the flags that show you who you are as a new creature in Christ Jesus. The old has slipped away, and you've been made new. You're no longer subject to the things of this world or the old man; you've been given new life through Christ Jesus.

These little words in God's amazing, incomparable Word tell us about the reality of who we are because of Jesus, but simply knowing them is only part of it. We must *know* Him as we are known—that means relationship. You can have relationship because Jesus made a way to the Father for you. So unlike the Pharisees, you are not limited to just knowing *about* God. You can actually *know God!* We know Him intimately because He has placed His Holy Spirit within us, and He connects us to the heart of God in a breathtaking, world-changing way. Praise God! Hallelujah! Thank you, Jesus! Amen!

Now, as you know Him better and better—not just about Him, but really knowing Him—the next stage I encourage you to enter is *sharing* that with those around you. We're called to invite people to let them see a living Christ in us. All around you are Christians living under-powered lives; lives of less than the abundant life that Jesus died to give them. They have yet to learn who they are in Christ. So as you learn, as you connect, as you grow—share it. Go and show and pour out to others, so that they too begin to learn the new creation realities made possible because of the finished work of Jesus Christ, our Lord, Savior, and the firstborn among many brothers and sisters. He showed us the way. Now it is our turn to go and show the world the love of God and what it means to be a man or woman who is living in Christ.

Terry Mathews Ministries

PO Box 3589 CORRALES, NM 87048

E-mail: terrymathews@msn.com

Visit us on the web: www.terrymathews.org

TERRY MATHEWS MINISTRIES

Books & Music CD's

BOOKS

HEALING IS FOR YOU

Many Christians struggle to receive healing. Many aren't sure if God wants to heal them while others aren't sure how to receive healing. In this powerful book you will discover the truth that God wants you well.

REJOICE IN HOPE

The message in this book will give clarity and insight into living an overcoming life.

MUSIC CD'S

All these CD's are full of original anointed prophetic songs that will strengthen your life and encourage your faith.

GOD IS ABOUT TO TURN SOME THINGS AROUND

DANCING IN THE FIRE

BRAGGIN' ON THE BLOOD

TIME TO PRAISE

SHOUTING GRACE

ACKNOWLEDGMENTS

Special thanks to:

My wife Angel.

My daughter, Joy and her husband John Peace; their daughters Mikaela and Maegann; their son, Mathew.

My daughter, Carrie and her husband Jeremy Dodge; and their son, Judah.

Anne Bahm, who greatly helped with this manuscript.